minimalist MARKETING

5

minimalist
MARKETING

How Entrepreneurs and Nonprofits are Reaching Their Audience

Without a Marketing Budget

JOE FONTENOT

Five Round Rocks Media

2018

Printed in the United States of America. For information, address Five Round Rocks Media, LLC, 848 Matador Dr, Gretna, LA 70056.

Artwork design by Joe Fontenot, with design input from Samuel Fontenot and Gary Myers.

First Five Round Rocks Media paperback edition: June 2018
First Five Round Rocks Media hardback edition: June 2018
ISBN 978-0-9981007-4-6 (hardback)
ISBN 978-0-9981007-3-9 (paperback)

Published by Five Round Rocks Media, LLC
www.FiveRoundRocks.com

"Never try to fool children, they expect nothing, and therefore see everything."

- HARRY HOUDINI

To Graham (5) and Hadley (3) who always see.

foreword i

By Wes Gay

introduction 1

What is marketing. The power of switching to minimalist marketing. And if marketing will help your brand.

Part 1: Strategies

chapter one: focus 16

The psychology of simple and the curse of knowledge. Why you're better if you stay in your lane. Don't try to solve your problems. And building on the model of the long tail.

chapter two: value 37

How to position your brand (and why you should). And why just about everything depends on finding a blue ocean.

chapter three: communication 64

Why your brain likes story. Steps to telling your brand's story in a way grows your business. And how to write words people want to read.

chapter four: direction 92

The fallacy of logic. The problem your audience is having with your brand. And the role of persuasion, pre-suasion, and manipulation in your marketing.

Part 2: Tactics

chapter five: scarcity 126

The bandwidth tax. The rules of scarcity. And a case study of Starbucks' most popular latte.

chapter six: gamification 135

How the five elements of game will change your business. Game theory versus gamification. And how Nike used Nike+ to rebound their image.

chapter seven: content marketing 142

How much should you give away for free. Things that make content marketing fail. And how Scott Adams uses Dilbert and politics to build his business.

chapter eight: sales funnel 149

The five step path to purchasing every customer goes through. What is a sales funnel and do you need one if you don't 'sell' things? And if you do, how do you build it? A case study of MailChimp's sales funnel.

chapter nine: price 165

Using anchoring, the goldilocks zone, and language to determine your prices.

*How to price products vs. services. Pricing for nonprofits and churches. And JC
Penney and their pricing fiasco.*

chapter ten: website 175

Your website's primary job. And the 10 laws of building a good website.

chapter eleven: word of mouth 188

*The secret to word of mouth marketing. And a case study of the 15 million
dollar comedian no one knows.*

chapter twelve: new audiences 198

*Using paid ads, sharing audiences, and finding brand ambassadors. The
nature and formula of going viral. And a case study of Spotify starting at zero.*

chapter thirteen: creating a marketing strategy 211

*The strategic formula. And how to build the three parts of your marketing
strategy.*

Glossary of Terms 224
Recommended Reading 228
Resources 232
Acknowledgements 234
Research 236

foreword

Imagine the scene: thousands of hungry people, but no food.

The leaders panicked. Those in attendance gave an entire day to be here. Men, women, children. All of them came to listen, but no one thought to prepare lunch. No one expected to still be here.

With the best of intentions, some leaders huddled in private to develop a plan. They reassessed the situation, reviewed the options, and knew what to do next.

Or so they thought.

Their genius idea wasn't so genius.

Because when Jesus asked the disciples what they had, they immediately responded with how much money was with them. That sum wouldn't buy food for the 15,000 to 20,000 in attendance.

These men made a common mistake: assuming a question about resources was limited to financial means. An accurate count of the treasury seemed like the right response. That's what you and I would do, right?

But Jesus knew that wasn't the right answer. Bringing enough money to the table wasn't the correct approach. If they had all the financial means in front of them to solve the problem, then a miracle doesn't happen.

Instead, when given a second chance to answer the question, they showed their resourcefulness. In other words, they showed a willingness to take their limited amount of non financial means and see what could be done.

And boy were they shocked.

The story of Jesus feeding the 5,000 is a great example of the power of resourcefulness over resources. It's tempting to fall into the trap that says you need more resources to accomplish something great.

After all, you need a bigger budget if you want to tell more people what you do, right?

Wrong.

That's what we assume in our church or non-profit. If we just had more money like the big companies, we'd be more effective. We'd put more in, so we inevitably get more out.

In my experience working with companies of all sizes, I've discovered one thing: the secret to reaching more people has nothing to do with resources. Too many businesses actually waste their dollars on things like marketing because they assume more resources equals more return.

It's more about the decisions made in using those resources. In other words, resourcefulness.

This mindset of resourcefulness is one Joe lays out in the following pages. As someone who's an expert in guiding entrepreneurs, nonprofits, and churches in their marketing, he knows the key strategies and tactics that, while small, can deliver an enormous return.

He leads you through a simple roadmap that helps clarify a better approach to your reaching people through your marketing.

And by mixing timeliness principles with timely practices, he helps you and your team future-proof the marketing plan for your organization.

I worked in churches and non-profits for over a decade, and I grew up with a dad as a worship pastor. There are simply too many organizations doing life-changing work, yet they often get in their own way. Instead of mastering what they've been given, they complain over what they don't have.

The greatest creative moments come when we have the clearest boundaries. When our limited are clearly defined, it forces us to make the most of what we have. That's not our default, though, because it's hard. It requires the sometimes arduous task of working hard with little so we can hopefully have more.

We need more churches and non-profits who master the ability to do more with little, to see something great come from something small. People out there need help, help only found in the good work you do. But they'll never know it exists if you don't know how to master resourcefulness in what you say and what you do.

Read this book, put it to work, and see the impact it has on your organization. It'll surprise you, and I can't wait to hear what happens.

- Wes Gay, Forbes Contributor & Marketing Consultant
Atlanta, 2018

what is marketing and is it for you?

I n its purest sense, marketing is simply bringing a product (or service) to market. If you have something of value, and if you have a specific group in mind that would benefit from that thing of value, then marketing is the process of connecting the two.

But that's pretty broad. And if we left it there, you could define everything from business accounting to supply-chain logistics as marketing.

Here's another definition, this one from the American Marketing Association. Marketing is "the activity, set of institutions, and processes for creating, communicating, delivering, and exchanging offerings that have value for customers, clients, partners, and society at large."

Other than being a mouthful, that's a pretty good definition. In concept, I agree. But I define it a little bit more straightforward. **Marketing** is the systematic process of getting the right message to the right audience. That's it.

It's *systematic* because it must start with a plan. Without a plan, all you have is a desire. And, while important, desire is not sufficient. I may have a desire to fly an airplane, but unless I study the discipline of aviation, I'm not going to make much progress. And so bringing something to market begins with a plan.

Next, it's about transmitting a *message*—not a product or service. The message will certainly contain the product or service, but the delivery of those parts, technically, fall under the area of operations. Marketing on the other hand is about communicating.

And finally, marketing revolves around paring the right message with the right *audience*. No single product or service is applicable to everyone. The more focused you are here, the more successful your efforts will be.

In truth, if you have a product you need to connect with an audience, then *you are a marketer*. Even if you're business card doesn't say "marketing," or if this is the very first marketing book you've read—you are still a marketer.

In this book we will look at how good marketers think. Throughout history, those who have succeeded have something that separates them from the rest. And that is the right mindset.

And that's what this book is about: Getting into the mindset of what *good* marketing is so that you can go out and *create* results.

what marketing *isn't*

The word "marketing" gets used a lot, so before we go any further it's good to take a look at a few of the things that marketing isn't.

Marketing isn't advertising

Perhaps the biggest misunderstanding of marketing is confusing it with advertising.

Advertising certainly falls *under* marketing. But a company doesn't have to do advertising to do marketing. Advertising is often associated with paying someone to put you in front of their audience.

As an example, consider the counter-example of word of mouth. Unlike in advertising, there's no one to pay in word of mouth. It's the result of making happy customers that voluntarily tell their friends about you. But word of mouth is a lot of intentional work. And, unless it's a fluke, it almost never happens on its own. It's a form of marketing that comes through building, not buying. And so if we limited our thinking of marketing to advertising, we'd be missing a lot of effective opportunities.

But the main reason why advertising is not equivalent to marketing is because the two are fundamentally different. Advertising is an outworking of your marketing, while marketing is the plan your advertising is based on. In other words, the marketing comes first and then the advertising follows.

Marketing isn't digital design or printed pieces

This is one I hear a lot. Someone will want to *see* your marketing. That's kind of like asking to see a company's business model. You can see different *parts* of it, or you can see a white paper describing it. But the actual thing is a concept.

This is similar to the note on advertising above. But this goes a step further. For instance, once your marketing is established, you'll create a **brand** (a logo, colors, and the like). Then you'll figure out where your audience resides and what they want to see. And finally, after all of this, you decide on the medium in which you will use to reach them.

The biggest problem with thinking about marketing like this is that you miss the strategic element. Without a strategy, you have no central *standard* for which to judge your efforts. For instance, similar businesses may be having great luck with a rebrand, or through mailing flyers to potential clients. And without a marketing strategy of your own, you'll be tempted to jump right in, because, after all, those things are working, right?

Maybe.

But there are a lot of questions you need to ask before you do that. The first two being: Where does this fit into my larger plan? And: Will it help more than what I'm currently doing?

Marketing isn't sales

In some respects, this is obvious. But drawing the line between the two can sometimes be difficult.

In general, sales is a front-line activity, and it's people-based. While marketing is a support function to sales, and it's systems-based.

The two are very closely related in business, and so they often get conflated. For instance, sales is people-based in that the salesperson's job is to close the deal. Marketing, on the hand, will dictate what group of people the salesperson should be talking to, as well as what key points they should be talking about. Because they work so closely, many businesses have a "Marketing and Sales" department.

Marketing isn't "Network Marketing" or "Multi-Level Marketing"

Network Marketing and Multi-Level Marketing just use the word marketing in their title. Other than that, they fall squarely in the category of sales.

Network, or Multi-Level, Marketing is often referred to as pyramid marketing. Say you're selling exercise supplements. You'll sell the supplements to people who want to use them, but in the process, you'll recruit *other* salespeople who will sell on your behalf. Now when these new salespeople sell something, you get a cut. And so you make money from what you sell directly, as well as from what those under you (in the pyramid) sell.

If the ratio of how much a salesperson makes from recruiting versus direct selling gets out of line, it can tip into an illegal area, often called a "pyramid scheme."

But on the legal end of things, some salespeople are quite adept at this kind of work, and will do well for themselves. And that's great.

But, despite the name, this isn't marketing. It's pure sales.

two philosophies of marketing

A person's worldview is a series of beliefs used to interpret the world. All data passes through a filter (their worldview) and is interpreted accordingly. In marketing, there's a similar concept. There are two different philosophies—or lenses—with which you can view everything you encounter. And depending on which philosophy you choose will depend on the kind of results you see.

The first philosophy of marketing is what I call **flat marketing**. It is essentially marketing based on advertising. People who confuse marketing with advertising, design, or print pieces are practicing flat marketing.

The problem with flat marketing is that it is very easy to spend a lot of money, but very difficult to track any of its progress. This is because there is rarely a *central idea* that's driving our marketing. As a result, when someone plops a great new idea down in front of us, our inclination is to pick it up and start using it. If you practice this philosophy you'll spend a lot of time chasing new things. And because of this, these kinds of marketers often do not have a lot of confidence in their approach.

The second philosophy of marketing is what I call **integral marketing**. This is a strategic form of marketing that begins with your product or service. Traditionally, the marketing department is *given* a thing, told its virtues, and then instructed to launch it out into the marketplace.

Integral marketing takes a few steps back. Before a product or service is designed, the needs and wants of the ideal audience are understood. Then, marketers work with the product development team, as well as the operations team, to build the right product.

The benefit of integral marketing is that by the time the product or service is available, it's merely a matter of letting the right people know about it. The rest takes care of itself.

This book is about the second philosophy: integral marketing. By stepping back and looking first at your audience's needs and then building (or changing) your product to meet them where they are, marketing is less of an endeavor and more of a result.

For this reason, this book will sometimes step out of the traditional areas of marketing and look more broadly at your business itself.

so, what is *minimalist* marketing?

The 80/20 principle says that 80% of the output (or results) comes from only 20% of the input (work). Ideally, if you can find that 20% and focus on it first, then you are already 80% to your finish line.

If you can further optimize the rest, you can create your 100% output on far less than 100% input. This, in a nutshell, is the art of business.

If I sell everything I acquire at exactly the same price I paid for it, then there's no margin, and I won't be able to keep my doors open for very long. I need to be more efficient than the rest of the market in *acquiring* product so that when I sell it to the market, I have money left over. That's called profit.

In the 1960s and 70s, marketing began to become a priority in corporations. Marketing departments were created and given budgets. And that worked well. For a time.

Now, however, people are tired of being marketed to. Traditional methods just don't work like they used to. And so if we're to continue communicating effectively with our audience, we need to *think* about marketing differently.

This is what **minimalist marketing** is about.

Like its name implies, it is about *less*. But the "less" does not mean less effort. Instead, the less refers to less budget. Or, rather, less of what the budget has traditionally gone toward. It's for this reason smaller companies who have virtually no marketing budget are able to not only compete with larger corporations, but, in many cases, win.

Paid advertising—previously the cornerstone tool of marketing departments—is seeing fewer and fewer returns. The market is simply saturated with advertisements, and it doesn't want any more.

Instead, what we see people responding to is *people*-oriented outreach.

If all a brand does is pay for Facebook ads, but never puts in the time to interact with their customers, they will almost always see low returns. But when they take the time to engage, they create an audience—an *engaged* audience—who is interested in them, and wants to hear more.

Minimalist marketing—and this book—is about the people-side of marketing. It's about creating relationships that people value. And when your audience values you, they buy from you.

strategies vs tactics

The original meaning of strategy was from the battlefield; it meant 'the art of the leader'—back then, generals. Strategy was how you deployed your resources; tactics were how battles were fought. Today leaders need to generate strategies that make sense in whatever larger systems they operate in—a task for outer focus.

- DANIEL GOLEMAN, Bestselling author of *Focus* and *Emotional Intelligence*

Strategies are principles that are always in play. Whatever you are doing, your strategy is relevant. For instance, if one of your longterm goals is to save enough for retirement, then you know that you will need x number of dollars by x time.

Tactics, on the other hand, are like tools in your belt. If I'm saving for retirement, I may choose to buy a house to build equity, or I may want to max out my 401(k). Or, I may do none of that. I may spend my time building a business I can later sell.

With tactics, the question is not: Is this right or wrong? Instead, the question is: Is this inline with my strategy?

Tactics are more concrete—like choosing to max out my 401(k) instead of building a business I can sell—while strategies are better thought of as ideas (I need to have x dollars by x time). Because of this, it's tempting to copy *tactics* of successful organizations, because we can see exactly what they did. But if that tactic does not align with your own strategy, it will often be a bad move for you.

The better option is to first understand your strategy—what is your finish line, and when (or how) are you going to get there? And *then* you can evaluate tactics.

will this book tell me how to do marketing?

Yes and no.

Can a General back at basecamp tell a sniper, buried in the field, what to do? Yes: "find the target and take him out." But *how* exactly should the sniper do that? And *when* is the right time? These are decisions the sniper in the field has to make, based on the information only he has access to.

You are the sniper.

Yes, this book will tell you what you should do. But it won't be able to tell you *how* to do it. Or *when*. Those are decisions that are different for every single person.

The good news is, if you understand *what* you should be doing, the *how* and *when* will take care of themselves.

what's in this book?

Part One covers the four strategies of marketing. Part Two looks at tactics, or practical applications of the strategies from Part One. Think of Part One as the principles that will apply to everything you do, while Part Two is the tools. You may or may not use every tool, depending on what you're trying to accomplish.

Part One is meant to be read in order. It builds on itself, and it is interdependent. Part Two on the other hand is more of a reference guide. You can read the chapters out of order. So once you get to Part Two, feel free to skip around, depending on where you are in your marketing.

Throughout the book I'll reference important graphs or templates. And as much as possible, I'll provide you with links to go and download them. (I use some of them on a regular basis, and others are spreadsheets you can modify.)

Also, when reading, you'll come across important terms; they'll be **bolded** for easy reference. They are also listed and defined in the glossary in the back of the book.

And speaking of terms, there is one in particular we should talk about now. I use the word **audience** through out the book in a specific way. This is the equivalent of your customer base. But "customer" is a bit too narrow. Your audience may be members of your church, or the community your nonprofit is built around, or simply traditional paying clients. Whatever the case, they are *the group you are trying to move to action.*

Here is what's in the book, chapter by chapter:

Chapter One is about **focus**. It may feel more like business than marketing. But these foundations are core to minimalist marketing —the kind of marketing that doesn't require a massive advertising budget.

Chapter Two looks at the nature of **value**. Much of value is about positioning, both in your message and your place in the market. This chapter leans on **Blue Ocean Strategy**.

Chapter Three—once you've established your focus (chapter one) and value (chapter two)—we'll look at crafting **your message**. A great message without a solid product behind it won't do you much good. In the same way, a good product without an effective message will disappear into obscurity.

Chapter Four is the control, or **direction**, of everything you've done up to this point. How do you influence your audience to pause their busyness and pay attention to you?

The remaining chapters are shorter and more focused on specific topics. Briefly:

Scarcity is the notion that limitations grab attention more so than non-limitations do.

Gamification is applying to your marketing the principles of what makes games attractive.

Content marketing is allowing people to ride for free so that when you do charge, it's to fans who are glad to pay.

A **sales funnel** is the intentional process by which you move your audience from the periphery to the point of purchase.

Price, more than the dollar sign, looks at our beliefs about money (and its impact on our marketing).

Your **website** isn't a repository of your company, it's an employee with one specific job.

Word of mouth, on the other hand, is the most powerful form of advertising—it cannot be bought, but it can be created.

Finding **new audiences** is a brief overview of how to expand your current audience base.

Finally, the last chapter is about how to create a **marketing strategy**. Your marketing strategy is your guide post for every dollar, minute, and piece of social capital you spend. It will tell you if you are moving in the right direction, or if you're heading into a cul-de-sac with no outlet. Here I'll walk you through how to create one, and give you free templates so you can download and build your own.

is this book for you?

I'll do one of those things where I ask you a question in return: Do you have good work that would benefit a specific audience if they knew about it? If the answer is yes—or if you *want* the answer to be yes—then, yes: this book is for you.

If, on the other hand, you're looking for a book that will tell you exactly what to do—an easy button—then no, this is not for you. If marketing were easy, there would be no need for books like this. And everyone would be doing it at maximum capacity.

But it's not easy. And it sometimes takes hard thinking. But the good news is, there are people (like the scores I've included in these pages) who do this day in and day out, and who are willing to guide you through the process.

If you're ready to start thinking about your marketing in a new way, a way that works and doesn't require a massive advertising budget, then let's get started.

Part 1:

strategies

The concepts that drive our execution

focus

What is it about some brands that allow them to succeed in the market? After all, everyone's budget is limited. No one gets *carte blanche* from the board. But, yet, some are still pulling far ahead of the rest.

There's a principle we learn from the everyday physics of a knife blade. The blade cuts because all of the force of the knife is focused onto a very small area. The more concentrated the focus, the less effort it takes to cut.

Cal Newport, who wrote his latest book *while* working toward tenure at Georgetown University—which if you're unfamiliar with the academic world: writing a book and working toward tenure at the same time is a slightly insane combination—compared focus to a "super power." Ironically, the more you limit yourself (the more you say *no*), the more force you have.

This is the power of focus.

But many organizations don't do this.

One reason is that saying *no* feels more like losing than saying *yes*. It takes a clear understanding of what the finish line is (and is *not*) in order to say no and still feel good about it. And without a clear finish line, boundaries are difficult to maintain.

When it comes to successful marketing, focus is the necessary first step. Without focus, you'll blow through your ad budget, but without anything notable to show for it at the end of the year. Without focus, you'll find yourself current on all of the latest marketing techniques, but you won't have any real understanding of how these shiny new things help *you* move forward.

In a way, focus is the art of saying no. But we only say no to some things so that we can say yes to better ones. The rest of this chapter looks at the benefits and techniques of bringing the right kind of focus into your marketing.

the psychology of simple

At the moment you perceive it, the snap has already come and gone. Your perceptual world always lags behind the real world.

- DAVID EAGLEMAN, Neurologist and author of *Incognito: the Secret Lives of the Brain*

On the personal level, simplicity makes us happy.

Psychologist Mihaly Csikszentmihalyi showed us this through his pioneering work of **flow**. This is the state where time disappears and you are completely consumed with what you are doing. In other words, life gets a lot simpler. The normal thoughts that pop into your brain and the external distractions seem to, temporarily, disappear.

In order for a person to get into the state of flow, they need to be doing something they enjoy, that engages them, and that has meaning. Without this three-prong criteria, flow is unlikely. And without flow, life goes back to busy and distracting.

As psychologist Daniel Goleman in his book *Focus* has noted: "Full absorption in what we do feels good, and pleasure is the emotional marker for flow."

Think about the implications of this for marketers. If we can make people *enjoy* our product or service, and if we can *align* it with meaning in their own life, and if we can then make it *accessible* enough for our audience to easily use it, then we can effectively *engineer* flow.

If this seems far fetched, it's not. Think about IKEA. If you've never been to an IKEA store, it's an experience in itself. It is a multi-floor maze of furniture, displays, and ridiculously cheap deals (my wife once picked up directional clip-on lights for $0.25 each).

They have child-care, so you can spend some peaceful time walking through their store—and if you're a parent, this alone is enough to sell you. And once you've burned a bunch of decision-making-calories, you can visit their own cafeteria-style restaurant that has, just like their furniture, its own exotically named food. (They have a pear-flavored soda, which, in my experience, was fun to try, but not to drink. However, the köttbullar meatballs are excellent. Pro tip.)

On top of this, their furniture is of the put-it-together-yourself variety. Some have complained about the headache of doing this, counting it as a strike against them. And for some, it might be. Their instructions, after all, are all pictures and no words.

But this DIY component does more than cut costs for IKEA. "Effort gives us the feeling of ownership, the feeling that we've created something," writes psychologist Dan Ariely and Jeff Kreisler. "After we invest effort in almost anything we feel extra love toward that thing we had a part in creating." In an article in the *Journal of Consumer Psychology,* this phenomenon was officially dubbed "the IKEA Effect."

But this is really just reflective of the larger issue of how our brains process information. Most of our brainpower is devoted to unconscious activity, things hidden from our conscious, analytical mind. In his research on the unconscious mind, Leonard Mlodinow notes that "deep concentration causes the energy consumption in your brain to go up by only about 1 percent. No matter what you are doing with your conscious mind, it is your unconscious that dominates your mental activity."

If most people are unconsciously making decisions, then what does that mean for us as marketers? Mlodinow explains, "categorization is a strategy our brains use to more efficiently process information." And "when you come up with an explanation for your feelings and behavior, your brain performs an action that would probably surprise you: it searches your mental database of cultural norms and picks something plausible." Neuroscientist, David Eagleman, has confirmed this in his own research, noting that "the brain generally does not need to know most things; it merely knows how to go out and retrieve the data"

In other words, by focusing on a specific task we increase the strength of the category that task is in. And because our brains think in terms of categories, the subconsciously "easy" decision is to go with a known category.

What this means for us as marketers is that the more we can put our good work into *recognizable categories*, that require some form of active engagement from our audience, the easier and *more likely* it will be for our audience to buy in—even without them consciously understanding why.

The concept of categories is one we see in our conscious lives as well. When you meet someone new, after exchanging names, what is almost always the next question to come up: "What do you do for a living?" When we ask this, we're putting them into a category: doctor, engineer, customer service rep. These categories become the filters we use to understand everything else we learn about them. Categories are such an integral part of our lives, they affect everything from home insurance ("rental," "single-family dwelling" "firewall") to book sales (in 2000, the *New York Times* created a "children's best sellers" list due primarily to the *Harry Potter* series dominating their normal best-seller list).

But if categories are such an imbedded—and even automatic—part of our life, why mention them here? Shouldn't they take care of themselves?

As it turns out, at least in the discipline of marketing, they don't. In fact, something quite the opposite happens.

the curse of knowledge

In their book, *Made to Stick*, Chip and Dan Heath discuss a form of cognitive bias called the **curse of knowledge**. This is the temptation "to use language that is sweeping, high level, and abstract."

And while we all recognize this language when we hear it, few of us recognize it when we're the ones speaking it. "When a CEO urges her team to 'unlock shareholder value,' that challenge *means something vivid to her.*"

This is because the curse of knowledge is often the result of a short-cut. The CEO understands what "unlock shareholder value" means, and so she uses it as a summary statement. It's the result of a lot of planning and background preparation and experience. And in her mind, it's a perfect summation. However, for everyone else, it's just meaningless jargon.

As business people who intimately understand our products or services, it's easy to fall into this trap. We know all of the background details and selling points, and so we summarize them into categories *we* understand. And what makes the curse of knowledge especially difficult to overcome is that it is *technically* a very accurate summation.

But the problem with the curse of knowledge is not its accuracy, it's that those hearing (or reading) it don't have the background knowledge to *understand* its accuracy. If our audience isn't connecting with what we're saying, then it doesn't matter how valuable it is—it's not working.

The antidote to the curse of knowledge comes in the form of translating to something tangible. And as with all translations, some parts will be lost.* But when we take the extra step of

---

* As a humorous example—and perhaps a bit legendary—a popular Pepsi jingle in the early seventies included the words "It's got a lot to give to those who like to live, cause Pepsi helps 'em come alive." Legend comically has it in the Chinese market this was translated to "Pepsi will bring your ancestors back from the dead." Fortunately, most translation errors are not this dramatic.

translating, we gain something much more valuable: audience understanding.

There are two ways to translate the curse of knowledge into something tangible. The first is to use an *analogy*. By picking out one such path for "unlocking shareholder value" (like, for instance, to create off-shoot products that fix the problems our shareholders have told us about), the concept of unlocking shareholder value is immediately understood.

The second antidote is to use story. One of the problems with the curse of knowledge is that we don't often realize we are doing it. We use jargon, because, to us, it's *not* jargon. It all has real meaning. We all know the story behind it.

But if we can (briefly) illustrate to our audience the story that started all of this, we will have solved our communication problem.

Story is a broad term. In business, however, it is a bit more narrow. **Story** is comprised of (1) the problem that needs to be solved, (2) the solution that solves the problem, and then (3) the success we've experienced as a result. (This three-part overview will be expanded in more detail in chapter three.)

By providing the story or known analogies (or both) in conjunction with your summary statement, you will protect your message from falling prey to the curse of knowledge.

staying in your lane

If you could choose between being good at most things in your field or being excellent at only one thing, which would you choose?

I'll grant you, it's a hard choice.

Being good at most things means your net is wide. And your audience will be potentially quite wide, too. However, being excellent at only one thing means you'll be better than everyone else. At least in that one area. Yet, your area of focus wouldn't appeal to nearly as many people. So, if you had to, which would you choose?

Your answer is important.

If you choose the first, you're a generalist. Kind of like a handyman. Nothing wrong with that. You can do just about anything. If someone has a problem with their sink? You can fix it. Toilet? Got it covered. A bit of shingles falling off the roof? Yep, that too. The problem with a generalist is that it doesn't take much to get *good enough* in each area. For instance, in the case of marketing, you may know your way around Adobe's Create Suite well enough to put together an ad or design a logo. Or perhaps you've built a few websites on Wordpress or SquareSpace, so you know how to set these things up. It's okay to charge for these services. But a generalist will never pull in top dollar, because there are a load of other people who can, after a short while, get to exactly where you are. The market is wide for generalists, but there is also a lot of competition.

If, on the other hand, you chose the second option—to be excellent in a single area—then congratulation, you're an *expert*.

Here's the secret about being an expert. The more you know in your area of expertise, the less you know about other things; ironically though, the more of an expert you are, the more people *trust you* in those other, non-expert areas.

Take for instance the PhD. In America this is the highest academic degree you can attain. While writing your dissertation you learn more than, in some cases, anyone else in the entire world about a minute sliver of an already narrow subject. Yet, having a PhD is an entrance requirement for all kinds of things, like, college professor (though you'll almost never teach on your dissertation, your area of expertise), or, keynote speaker at academic conferences (though, again, see above). There's absolutely nothing wrong with having a PhD. It's a worthy pursuit. My point is that once you have this extraordinarily narrow expertise people will look at you more valuably in all sorts of *other* areas.

This is the power of the expert.

But PhDs are not the only kinds of experts. Anyone who focuses their time and work in a single area, testing their results, and making regular improvements is an expert. Mike Rowe, host of Discovery Channel's *Dirty Jobs,* is an expert on the America blue collar work force. Walt Disney was an expert showman. Alfred Hitchcock an expert director. And Bono an expert singer. My dad, even, he's an expert programmer, and my friend Marilyn is an expert writer.

Does it mean that any of these people are the *best* at these things?

No. Their expertise is not a function of their absolute value in the world, as if expertise were some kind of ranking system. Rather, their expertise is such because this is the *main* thing they are known for.

(As an aside, and something we'll cover more in the next chapter: being an expert in one area does not mean that you cannot be an expert in other areas. Think of it more as a priority. You are known for X. But you are also proficient in Y, and so when someone contacts you for X, you can steer the conversation toward

Y, too. They still probably won't think of you for Y. All they'll remember is that they came to you and you fixed their problems.)

The temptation here is to spread your net wide. *Don't turn down anything. You never know when you'll have another chance.* The sad, other side to this coin is that when you throw your net wide, it spreads open, and the holes show through. And despite your best efforts, you miss a lot.

To become valuable in the market, you need to be an expert, not a generalist. Your business needs to be clearly defined in the market as the go-to place for X.

Own your expertise. Focus isn't leaving anything on the table. In fact, the opposite is quite true. Most of what will open up to you will come with focus—not the other way around.

quit trying to solve your problems

A good advertisement is one which sells the product without drawing attention to itself.
- DAVID OGILVY, known by many as the father of advertising

I'll start with the bad news: nobody but you cares about your problems.

That's harsh, I know. But in a strange way, it's also good news. If you're the only one that cares about *your* problems, then likely the same holds true for your audience. They are first and foremost interested in *their* problems.

And as obvious as all of this sounds, it's not. Think about how many business websites you've visited that spend all of their space talking about *them*selves, *their* history, and *their* achievements. Or, how many ads you've seen that are all about the company and *its* virtues. On some level, these things sound right. An ad for baby washcloths should be about, well baby washcloths, right?

Actually, *no*.

Take a look at the box for Johnson's baby washcloths (see figure 1.1 below).

What is their product about? It's not about washcloths. It's about a happy and healthy baby, who, in turn, has a *happy and healthy mom*. Positionally, their product is nothing more than the vehicle to get you to that happy, healthy place. In other words, it isn't about them, it's about *you*.

Contrast this with Johnson's real problem. They need to sell enough products to keep shareholders happy, and they need to keep their unit costs low (so as not to mess with their profit margins). In the process, they need to make sure their manufacturers are maintaining their own high standards so that the moms who use their products will like them enough to recommend them to their other mom-friends. I can guarantee you: this—their pain—is the topic of conversation swirling around board meetings at Johnson's.

But this is not what comes out in their marketing. Here is what the back of this same box reads:

"We love babies. And we understand their delicate skin and eyes are sensitive. That's why our unique No More Tears hair and body wash formula is designed to be gentle enough to cleanse sensitive newborn skin without drying. It's dermatologist-tested, dye-free, and soap-free. Johnson's Baby brand, the #1 choice in hospitals and at home."

As a copywriter, it would be my utter delight to dissect every line of this for you. This is great copy. But I'll do my best to live up to this chapter and just stay *focused* to how they deal with their customer's problem.

Notice their start: they love what you love. Or, the reverse, they want to make sure your number-one pain (pain to your baby) never happens. They even go so far as to name their 'unique' formula, "No more tears."

But also notice how they *do* talk about themselves. Once they've established that their biggest problem is your biggest problem, they move on to show how they are well qualified to be the ones to solve that problem for you. (More on how to talk about yourself in chapter three.)

And this highlights an important point: the focus of your marketing needs to be on the *overlap* of their pain and your expertise (see figure 1.2 below).

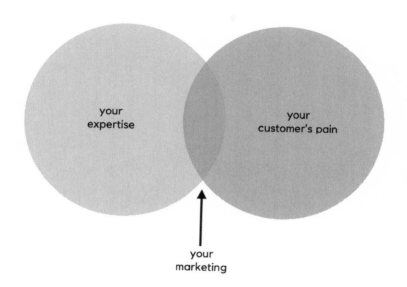

your
marketing

Johnson's has a lot of expertise: their R&D; how many industry-leading patents they hold; how many health issues they've solved; even how well they do their marketing (after all, good marketing is the service of putting the right work in front of the right people at the right time, and as a consumer, that's valuable). But they don't talk about any of that. The only expertise they talk about is what directly intersects with their customer's pain. And they only do it after they've established everything else.

In the ad above, this is where they reveal to their audience that Johnson's is the number one choice in *hospitals* (a higher, and regulated, standard) and homes. Starting with that is boastful and off-putting. But finishing with it—after everything else has been established—is comforting.

The Marketing Mindset

A client of mine, David, owns the Idea Factory in New Orleans where he sells high-end wooden toys out of his French Quarter shop. Beyond offering something unique to travelers (a market crowded with identically cheap t-shirts and shot glasses), he also solves a pain point.

One of his customers is a businesswoman who regularly hosts high-end dinner-parties for some of her key clients. She will often buy pieces from the Idea Factory to give out as gifts at her parties. Her guests are well traveled and can be a bit jaded. Because a lot often rides on these dinners, it's important that she makes a good impression. These high-end novelty toys give her the opportunity to do just that.

David's good at finding unique wooden pieces. But that's not what he sells.

What he really sells is *access*.

By tapping into his customer's deeper needs and desires, he's able to provide a unique product that fits a specific problem. He's able to help them get somewhere they could not get on their own.

If he were only selling unique toys, someone could always come behind and undercut him. Commodity- (or feature-) based marketing is a race to the bottom.

On the other hand, this kind of customer's-problem-first mindset of marketing provides you a roadmap for how you do all of your outreach. If every product, ad, or message created had to first pass this test: how is this solving my customer's problem? would you ever put out anything your customer doesn't want? Of course not. When we look at focused, successful brands, we see regular patterns. And one of those patterns is that when they talk about themselves, it's primarily at the intersection of their customer's pain and their expertise to solve that pain.

The rest of the chapter follows the mechanism that allows *non-*industry leaders (and smaller businesses in general) to put this customer-pain-expert-solution model into action.

the long tail

For many, globalization is a dirty word.

Globalization is what's shifted jobs overseas. It's what's allowed competitors like Walmart to get such low unit costs. And it's what's made local mom-and-pops fall almost unanimously to online shopping empires.

But globalization in itself isn't a bad thing. It's just a *new* thing. And like all new things, if we don't play by the new rules, we'll find ourself out of the game.

I've seen many marketers try to fight globalization by claiming local value. Don't buy X, buy Y, because it's "made right here." But this local appeal usually only works for artisan products, where craftsmanship is forefront in the product. And even then, the fact that the craftsman is local needs to be germane to the product itself, like Ozarka, the bottled water "Made in Texas." Their water comes from three springs, all located in Texas.

But if you're pushing "buy local" for a commodity, like toilet paper or tooth brushes—something that can easily be found online for cheaper—then there's no reason (beyond charity) to actually pay more and buy local.

And this is the heart of the mom-and-pop problem. With globalization comes access. And with access comes lower prices or more options (or both). Previously mom-and-pops relied on a geographic barrier. Their audience was captive, and so it made the most sense to buy local. But not anymore.

Does this mean mom-and-pops are out of luck?

No. Far from it, in fact.

Mom-and-pops (and by extension: entrepreneurs in general) have something the larger Amazons and Walmarts do not: and that's the ability to move *quickly*. The leaders are dinosaurs. They're big. They weigh a lot. And so they can do a lot of damage when they move. But they're not nimble. When they do move, it takes a lot energy. And, likewise, when they need to change, that takes time and energy, as well.

This is where globalization becomes a benefit.

We see this specifically in the notion of the **long tail**.

In statistics, the "tail" (see figure 1.3 below) is the area that has high variety with low volume. This is contrasted by the "head," which is the opposite: low variety with high volume.

In the book-selling world, an author like Josh Foer, who wrote the *New York Times* bestselling *Moonwalking with Einstein* (published by Penguin Books) would, statistically speaking, be in the head. Very few authors make it to a top publisher like Penguin or have a *NYT* bestseller, but when they do, there are high returns. Taking this further, an author like John Grisham would be even farther left into the head, to the point of being a household name. There are only a *handful* of these spots.

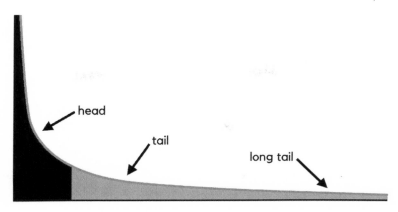

The opposite of this is the guys who run Sterling and Stone Publishers (sterlingandstone.net). They are three authors who self-publish, and together they write a *couple million* words per year. (To put that figure in perspective, the entire seven-part Harry Potter series was about a million words.) Their business model is to release a high *quantity* of books. No single book will be a blockbuster, but taken together, they sell a lot of books. And because they self-publish, they have a much higher margin on their books. This, combined with the high number of titles they release each year, allows them to pull in *overall* volume that would normally only come from a bestseller. In this way, they make a good living for themselves.

Sterling and Stone is an example of a long tail business.

The value the long tail brings to marketing is focus. You can now find a niche that would have never been profitable before. And in the long tail, you can create an entire business model out of it.

I have an entrepreneurially minded friend who's a fireman. A few years ago he had an idea for a new kind of measuring tape. So he applied for a patent, contracted a factory in China to build him 10,000 units, and then worked with a few local hardware stores to carry them on consignment. Pre-internet, this model would have been very difficult, if not impossible. Today the hardest part is coming up with the idea.

In his book, *The Long Tail*, Chris Anderson—the former editor in chief of *Wired* magazine (not to be confused with the Chris Anderson who runs the TED conferences)—explains the three forces behind why the long tail works so well. First, the tools of production have been democratized. What used to be held for the elite is now open to the public. Second, the cost of consumption has been cut. With the broadening of access came the lowering of prices. And third, the connecting of supply and demand. This is more a communication aspect than it is anything else, where there is a clear channel between the demand and the supply.

Force 1: Democratizing the tools of production
Pre-computer, when typewriters and pen and paper were standard, there was no way for an average person to create a professional looking product, like a book. Everything from design to layout and even the printing needed to go through a professional company (or series of companies) to bring the work to life. And then, as in the case of books, it required you to order a *lot* of them.

Now it's all different. An author can write an entire book on her computer, upload it to a company like CreateSpace or IngramSpark, and when someone is ready to purchase it, the book is created right then (with no need for inventory).

Without the right tools, the long tail is still just a statistical model, devoid from any practical business. Fortunately, tools like the personal computer have touched every form of marketing, from nonprofits and churches to manufacturer and service-based startups.

Force 2: Cutting Cost of Consumption

If the computer is part one, then the Internet is part two. The computer gave us access, but the Internet is what has allowed us to expand and use that access.

"The Internet," Anderson notes, "simply makes it cheaper to reach more people, effectively increasing the liquidity of the market in the Tail. That, in turn, translates to more consumption."

Amazon.com is a great place to see this in action. The majority of what is sold on Amazon is not actually from Amazon, it's from third-party sellers. People like you and me who have a specialized product, create an amazon seller account, and offer their wares to the world. If you're looking for something far out, a bit of radioactive uranium ore, for instance, you can get that for $39.95 with free shipping. How about a realistic replica of human fat for science class? No problem, you can get that *plus* a replica muscle tissue for only $46.25. Or—my personal favorite—1,500 live ladybugs. That's only $7.50 plus $3.49 shipping.

These examples are a bit absurd, but they illustrate the point: because of the long tail, anywhere your expertise aligns with your customers demands, there is a viable means for marketing it.

Force 3: Connecting Supply and Demand

This third force is an outworking of the first two.

Going back to the bookselling model for a moment: When the ability to self-publish became both democratized (force 1) as well as affordable (force 2), the gatekeepers shifted. No longer were the gatekeepers the high-end editors at name brand publishers. Now they're made up of algorithms and user reviews.

The first force established the long tail. The second force fattened it. And now the third now force fuels it. In the third force we see demand being *driven down* the curve from the head into the tail. "In other words," writes Anderson, "the third force further increases demand for the niches and flattens the curve, shifting its center of gravity to the right."

With the development of the third force, there is still a head. There will still be super-stars. But the chances for becoming a super-star become less and less. Conversely, however, the chance of making it in the long tail only increases.

The Long Tail and Marketing

Previously, you had to focus on a product or service somewhere in the head (a messy, competitive space). Or, if you were lucky, geography prohibited your audience from going elsewhere. But for most industries, globalization has removed the geography walls. And the competition for the head has only grown.

The more you can own a space—a niche—the more control you have. You are not a me-too brand, and, in many ways, competition diminishes, too. By stepping into the long tail, you can not only find a profitable business, but you can focus all of your marketing. As we'll look in the next chapter, the most *valuable* businesses are always focused businesses.

highlights

Focus is like a knife blade. It's small, but when all of your energy is concentrated on it, it makes a noticeable impact.

As humans we appreciate simplicity. It's where we derive pleasure. But it's also where we derive comfort. We see this in everything from our ability to learn to our ability to understand. We seek the simple, straightforward answer. As brands, the closer we get to this, the stronger we become in our audience's mind.

One outworking of this is the expert. When faced with being a generalist (wide) or an expert (narrow), the market responds disproportionately: it likes the expert more. The irony here, is that the market will ask the expert to do the generalists job, even though the expert is often less qualified. When you have a choice, become the expert.

The best place to focus is where your expertise overlaps with your audience's pain. By talking about your expertise in terms of their pain—or, to put it positively: their desire—you begin to 'speak their language.' This is simply a case of service. You are out to solve their problems, not yours.

Finally, the **long tail**. This is the economic engine that makes such a narrow focus possible. And not only possible, but profitable. The long tail is a statistical term. In the market, it represents the moving away from household names and into niche spaces. The two extremes have always existed, and they will continue to, but what we see is a flattening of the curve, where the middle ground is becoming more accessible and more profitable.

V alue is one of those things many claim, but few actually deliver.

Why is that? And what role does value play in marketing? Is it just a nice thing to know, but not critical to succeed? Or is it the cornerstone of your brand? And if it *is* your cornerstone, how much of that can your marketing deliver?

This chapter looks at these questions in the context of how your market *perceives* your value. This word perceives is important. It's not about fooling your audience. If you don't have the true value to back up your perception, you won't get far. It will only be a matter of time before the rest of the world finds out.

However, this is a case where the opposite is *not* true. Simply being good—or even great—is almost never enough to get you noticed. Instead, you have to be intentional about it. You have to let the market know in the right way about the value you offer.

This is the essence of value: being good while strategically *showing* that good. And it is the showing side that intersects with your marketing.

who cares?

Why are you special? And who cares?

For a lot of brands, these are scary questions. But the answers to these questions are behind the success of your marketing.

I have a client whose business is in decline. They are a national brand, and for decades their numbers were going up. But now they're not. And now they're trying to figure out why.

I'll let you in on the secret: They are years too late. There is still hope for them. But it's going to be a rough road back.

Twenty and thirty years ago, when they couldn't fail, they assumed their customers were attracted to *them*. They didn't stop to consider why their customers were actually buying. As it turns out, at that time the market highly valued what they were selling, and so it didn't really matter *who* was selling it. In other words, their customers weren't buying from them—they were buying from anyone. They rode the market's wave up thinking of themselves as a cause and not an effect.

But when the market changed, and when their customers' needs evolved, they stopped buying, and my client was caught completely off guard.

When times are good, you have to be brave or stupid (or a little of both) to mess with a good thing. That's the temptation that many, like my client here, face. And so who would mess with a good thing?

But there's another option.

That's to understand your success.

There's a superficial way to do this. And a lot of people fall into this. And that's to look at your success and then come up with reasons that support it. Social psychologist Robert Cialdini in his book, *Pre-Suasion*, talks about this. A form of this we often see manifested in business is when we credit CEOs with a company's success or decline (when in fact, the CEO has little to do with it).

"Business performance analyst have termed this tendency 'the romance of leadership'," notes Cialdini, "and have demonstrated that other factors (such as workforce quality, existing internal business systems, and market conditions) have a greater impact on corporate profits than CEO actions do; yet the leader is assigned outsize responsibility for company results."

The romance of leadership is a tempting trap to fall into. It's easy. It's a reasonable category, and, on the face of it, it makes sense. But if we really want to understand our success, we need to be able to pinpoint what will *increase* our results. If you truly understand *why* people are buying from you, then it's entirely likely that you can give them more of it and increase your demand.

In terms of the market, this is a question of being special. Are you a me-too brand that the market uses when its still hungry, but tosses aside as soon as its primary object of affection keeps it satisfied? Or are you something different? Something special that a segment of the market seeks out?

Special is hard. It takes a lot of work, and a lot of risk. But, in the end, that extra work (and risk) is what gives you a *choice*. Me-too brands ride the waves. When the market blows east or west—or doesn't blow at all—the me-too brands have no choice but to do what the market says. And when the market decides it doesn't have room for you any more, so much the worse for those brands.

But being special is different. To continue my wave analogy: special is the boat with the motor. It's what gives you the choice to follow—or not follow—the market.

And it's in this way that special creates its own *demand*. When you do the work to become special, categories are built around you. You're no longer a runner-up or a fill in. You *are* the attraction.

So, the question then is: how do you become special?

The answer to this question is by adding more value. Or, as it relates to marketing, by *showing* the market your added value.

The client I opened this section with, they're actually quite special. Their journey is not about building something special as much as it is understanding what already makes them so valuable in the market and then putting *that* above all else. For them, it's learning to think in a new way. If you've been around for a few years, then there's something that's kept you around. You're surviving for a reason.

The next section, positioning, is all about finding that something and putting it right out in front.

how to position yourself

Experiments have shown that the first is more likely to be believed.
- DANIEL KAHNEMAN, Nobel prize winner

In the market, your value is defined by *where* you are. So when it comes to standing out in a noisy marketplace, what is more important than your actual value is your *perceived* value.

This might sound like you don't have to have real value—that you only need people to believe you do—but that's not true at all. In fact, the opposite scenario is more likely to be the case. Many times competitors *do* have value. But the point is, value alone is not sufficient in marketing. The market has to recognize you as the owner, or leader, of that value.

Take the car manufacturer, Volvo, for instance. What do you think of when you think of Volvo? Safety. They've done a good job at **positioning** themselves as the safest car on the road.

But, in reality, *are* they more safe than other cars?

Perhaps, to some degree, they are. They pioneered the three point seat-belt and side-impact airbags. Safety seems to genuinely be their top priority. But these safety features were not only copied by their competitors, they have since, in many cases, been made *mandatory* by the government. Doesn't that, in effect, cause Volvo to lose their competitive position?

No.

In fact, it makes it stronger.

In 2001 Amazon positioned themselves as *the place* to find books. Here was their official positioning statement at the time:

"For World Wide Web users who enjoy books, Amazon.com is a retail bookseller that provides instant access to over 1.1 million books. Unlike traditional book retailers, Amazon.com provides a combination of extraordinary convenience, low prices, and comprehensive selection."

But here's the rub. Their books weren't "instant." They had to be shipped. And this was before the days of Amazon Prime. In 2001 it would usually take three to five days for your book to arrive. That's a lot longer than driving to a brick and mortar store and picking up a book. But this actually misses the point.

Their positioning strategy was to be your *complete* source of books.

They weren't selling hard to find books (though they undoubtedly had those). And they weren't selling price-matching (though their lack of traditional overhead would likely make their prices competitive). And they certainly weren't selling the fastest possible delivery service. They were selling one-stop shopping.

In the almost two decades since that statement, Amazon has expanded their offerings to include virtually everything. But notice, at least in 2018, their position is still the same. Today it reads: "Our vision is...to build a place where people can come to find and discover anything they might want to buy online." In other words, whatever you need, they've got it. They own this position.

The power of positioning is undeniable.

As a brand, how you position yourself will determine your market share. If you are a me-too brand, then you will get the left-over scraps and find yourself in a defensive position more often than not. But if you are a leader—if you position yourself well— then the market will reward you, as it does, with first picks and the prime of the market.

But how do you use positioning in marketing?

Positioning relies on three essential laws.

The first law is to be, well, first. In this game, second really is the first looser. First can take many shapes: you can be the first chronologically; you can be the first in size (biggest or smallest); or you can be the first in other ways (like price or convenience or technique).

The second law is that if you are not already first, then you must *become* first. In short this is about defining a new category. The traditional route for this is rarely successful ("work harder"), and so the second law is about building new spaces.

The third law is about branding: have a name with a clear identity. A name is focused, and it's known for *that* thing. A focus on too much dilutes who you are in the market. When this happens your position becomes ambiguous.

Volvo was the first to pioneer safety. Currently their goal is by 2020 to create a car that no one dies in. Amazon recently bought WholeFoods and has created instant re-order buttons you can stick all over your pantry or closet. It doesn't matter if competitors copy, Volvo owns safety, and Amazon owns convenient online shopping.

The question for you now is, how can you position *your* brand?

To get there, let's look a little closer at the three laws of positioning.

Law 1: Be First

In their seminal work on positioning, marketing godfathers Al Ries and Jack Trout note that "the easiest way to get into a person's mind is to be first."

Sometimes this means being literally first. Most of us know (or could guess) who has the most Olympic gold metals (Michael Phelps: 23). But do you know who has the second greatest number? Larisa Latynina, a Russian gymnast who retired in 1966. How about the first man on the moon? That's easy: Neil Armstrong. Every kid now grows up knowing that. But what about the second? And the tallest mountain? Or the tallest building? If you know these 'firsts' (and most of us do) the chances of knowing their 'seconds' is much slimmer.

But why is it that the first position is so much easier to remember than the second (or the third or fourth or fifth)?

Simply, there is no relevant category for anything after first.

As Peter Thiel notes in *Zero to One,* "Doing what we already know how to do takes the world from 1 to *n*, adding more of something familiar. But every time we create something new, we go from 0 to 1. The act of creation is singular, as in the moment of creation, and the result is something fresh and strange."

What's the difference between the second and the one-hundredth and second? Thiel's point is, categorically speaking: not much.

That's because the first changes things. Before it there was none. Every spot after first is just a duplication. Nothing else changes our world the way the first does.

But being first is not always about being chronologically first. The 'first' spot is often filled by the first brand to make a name for themselves—not necessarily the first to compete. Consider Apple's iPhone. In 2007, when the iPhone was introduced, there were other smartphones already on the market. The other smartphones had touch screens and apps that could access the internet. So how did the iPhone become known as *the* smartphone? Apple did it by owning the smartphone space.

In 2007, Apple didn't invent anything new. What they did was solve a quality-control problem the rest of the smartphone manufacturers couldn't. One of their closest competitors was the Blackberry Curve, which had a *text-based* web browser. Other touch screen phones were imprecise and slow, meaning you more often fat-fingered what you were trying to select, and then it took patience (slow) waiting on the phone to correct your error.

Apple took all of these features (none of which they were the first at) but then became the first to make them truly excellent. The web on the iPhone looked exactly like it did on your computer. The touch screen was amazingly accurate. And the phone was instantly responsive. More than that, their apps were easy to use. For the most part, no buried menus or lists to browse.

Being first is about being the first to *own a space* in the market. Until 2007, no one owned the smartphone space. There were other smartphones on the market, but none were as good as the iPhone. And so when Apple released the iPhone, the market responded. And because they were first to do it so well, the iPhone became known as the *standard* for smartphones.

Now, pick up any smartphone and look at it through squinted eyes. They all look the same, don't they? A vertical-oriented touchscreen with a grid of colorful apps. Apple is the leader, and everyone else is following.

Law 2: Become First

Admittedly, first is not always available—chronologically or otherwise. And when it is available, there's a lot of risk. Does the market really want this? Will they understand what we're doing here?

For many brands *becoming* first is a more realistic option.

If you will allow me once more, let's again look at the case of Apple. But this time let's look at the marketshare for their computers. How often do you walk into a coffee shop and see *at least* one of those glowing apples on the back of a laptop? How about in the airport? Or on a college campus? The iconic Apple MacBook is everywhere.

Or…so it seems.

I walked through the mall recently (a blessedly rare occasion), and the Apple store was packed. I counted over fifty employees. And there had to be at least two-hundred customers. Not too far away was the Microsoft store. It had the same unfinished light colored wood fixtures. (They even all wore matching red t-shirts.) But there were only about six employees standing around (and a single, lonely customer, who was in fact, actually walking out).

If we go by appearances, Apple is clearly wiping the floor with Microsoft.

But if we look at a different factor—their market share (how much of the market they have truly captured)—we couldn't see more of an opposite picture.

For some years now Microsoft has been holding around *ninety percent* of the market. Even up until the end of 2017, Windows comes in at 88.39% marketshare. Apple's OSX on the other hand struggles to break 10%. And quite a few times they've dipped below 7%.

There are a lot of ways to explain this data. Apple is a massive brand. In the last few years, their mobile devices have clearly outpaced their computers. But even still, their mobile marketshare hovers between 10-20%. (Google's Android owns the lion's-share of mobile at 80-90%.)

So what's the explanation?

How is it that Apple's OSX seems so ubiquitous, while Microsoft's Windows (and Google's Android) don't?

The answer is found in the second law of positioning.

While Apple's and Microsoft's history both go back to the very early days of personal computers, Microsoft was the clear winner of this market. They dominated. It wasn't until Jobs' second tenure at Apple that things began to change.

But it wasn't marketshare that changed (not to the level sufficient to knock Microsoft off their throne). Instead what Jobs changed was Apple's positioning.

Steve Jobs knew there was a market for people who didn't want to be like everyone else. He knew inventors and creators had an affinity for standing out, but also (typically) they weren't tech people. And so Jobs created two campaigns that defined Apple's position. "Think Different" and "It just works."

Apple successfully positioned themselves in a minority camp of the greats like Albert Einstein and Mahatma Gandhi. And then, contra Windows' plethora of hardware manufacturers, Apple built their own hardware and so better controlled the reliability. This was the foundation for their "It Just Works" campaign.

As a result—and their financials show it—Apple positioned themselves as a leader in both the desktop and tablet markets without even getting close to becoming the marketshare leader.

The seminal lesson here is, first is *relative* to the mind of your audience.

There's a story of the famous seventeenth century samurai, Miyamoto Musashi. In his lifetime he became legendary for winning over sixty duels. And for one of these he was attacked by ten opponents at the same time. This kind of outnumbering was unusual in samurai culture, but Musashi, as usual, was already ahead of his attackers. Instead of fighting them all at the same time, he positioned himself next to a tree so that his opponents had to come at him one at a time. By positioning himself according to *his advantage*, the leverage of his enemies evaporated. Musashi won the duel.

Law 3: Have a Name

All organizations have a name. But when it comes to positioning only a few have honed their reputation to a name that matters.

In the mind of your audience, to be memorable, you need to fit into a single category. Adobe makes creative software. REI equips outdoor adventurers. Forbes provides leading business news. And Google is for finding things. It doesn't matter that these companies do other things. (Adobe is in the process of launching a marketing service, while Google makes the vast majority of its income on advertising.) What matters is that in the minds of their audiences, this singular thing is what they're known for.

But what do you do when you don't have that one thing? What if you have multiple successful products or services on the market? How do you create a clear 'bucket' for your audience to put you in?

Proctor & Gamble is a company with just such a problem. With over sixty brands under their umbrella—everything from Crest to Vicks to Tide—they needed to find a way to simplify their image to their audience. And so they asked themselves: what is the unifying factor that draws all sixty-plus brands of P&G together?

The answer, as it turns out, is mom.

In 2012, to coincide with the summer Olympics, Academy award nominated Mexican director, Alejandro González Iñárritu, created a short film called "Thank You, Mom." In it, he focused on the pivotal role moms play in creating Olympic athletes.

One of the reasons the film was so powerful was that it followed the everyday (and often overlooked) work moms do to care for their children. It showed littles ones falling down and being picked back up again and comforted by their mothers. As the film progressed, the children got older. And instead of learning basic skills like walking, they were learning how to play with other children. Then, finally, they were training. Training against tremendous odds to make it to the Olympics. And, of course, mom was still right there with them, picking them up and encouraging them the whole way.

A theme in the film was that whenever we attempted something new (be it walking, playing, or training) we fall down. Success always comes with pain. But, through that pain, mom is there to help us back up so that we can keep pushing forward.

The film culminates with moms watching their now-grown-up little ones competing on the international Olympic stage. It's clear in the physical sense that they've outgrown their need for their moms. But it's also just as clear that these athletes owe everything they've accomplished to their moms.

To the ones that often get overlooked—but who most often work the hardest—P&G created their biggest (and perhaps most successful) campaign. It started with this short film. But, six years later, the campaign is still running (and growing).

P&G took a broad market reach (of over sixty brands) and found the theme that runs through them all: mom. Moms are the ones that primarily buy P&G's products, and so they decided to make them the hero of their marketing.

Creating a specific identify for your brand—the one thing that you do exceptionally well—becomes your spotlight to shine.

Without it, you're just another soon-to-be-forgotten noise in the middle of thousands, if not millions, of other noises squeaking for attention.

This is positioning.

But in many ways—and at risk of undoing everything I've just written—positioning *isn't* everything.

Think of positioning as working like a spotlight. If you shine your light on something unattractive, people won't magically *become* attracted to it. They'll just know faster that they're not interested.

If, on the other hand, you've got a good product and then take the time to shine your light on it, people *will* be attracted to it. This is what happened in the Microsoft store. Apple reaches a specific niche. Microsoft doesn't. Yet, they copied Apple's spotlight (the store, in this example), and they ended up shining a light on their weakness instead of their strength.

What's going on here is about something deeper. Positioning only works when you've got something good, because positioning is reflective of that deeper value.

So, what do you need to back up your positioning? This is to where we now turn: a blue ocean strategy.

finding a blue ocean strategy

The idea behind a blue ocean strategy is simple. The market operates much like the ecosystem of the ocean. Big sharks eat little fish. And when they do, the ocean becomes red. Full of blood and survival.

For the little fish to compete, they have to spend their time hiding from the big sharks, or learning (if such a thing is possible) how to become big sharks themselves.

Neither scenario is very attractive.

But this is how our market often shapes up. If you're the mom-and-pop, Walmart is eating you out of business. If you've created, patented, and produced a new product, it's only a matter of time before a bigger brand either buys you out or creates the same thing quicker and at lower cost.

The small business is the small fish. Waiting to be eaten by the big shark.

But being a small fish does not have to be an inherent weakness. If you can survive, there is a lot of value to being small. Enviable qualities, like agility, customization, and personalized service, to name a few, make smaller businesses more attractive to more people than larger faceless corporations.

But so often the small one wants to be the big one—not for the values of being big—simply just to survive.

The real question is, if you could survive small, would you?

I've worked with many entrepreneurs who have great businesses. They do not want to become a 1,000-or-more-employee corporation. They want to continue being a high-end boutique, or they want to keep serving their neighborhood with the level of service a 1-800 number could never do.

For them, building an empire is not the goal: creating good work for good people is.

But let's extend this idea, because it's not just small businesses getting eaten here. K-Mart was (and still is) a large corporation. And while they're still around, they didn't make it. Not really.

Why? Because they didn't provide an inherent value. They didn't set themselves apart as different in the market. Walmart made just-in-time inventory a reality for big box stores (meaning little local storage was needed and shelves were always stocked). K-Mart's shelves would often have large empty areas. And they didn't seem to understand how people shopped, so it was hard to find things.

As long as K-Mart was the largest "small" store, they were fine. The market was theirs. But as soon as another competitor came along with the same (and bigger) size—and then improved the small-store problems (inventory and placement)—K-Mart was done. They'd lost their competitive advantage.

How should a brand like K-Mart have protected them self from this? How does *any* brand—regardless of size—protect itself from this kind of competitor?

The answer is to become a blue ocean company.

In 2005, two professors from the INSEAD business school in France, W. Chan Kim and Renée Mauborgne, compiled a study of strategic moves, spanning more than thirty industries over a period of a century. Their findings were published in their book, *Blue Ocean Strategy.*

What they discovered was that there is a specific kind of successful company that doesn't depend on luck or funding. These kinds of companies have three things in common: they are divergent, focused, and can communicate.

Divergent is the core of blue ocean. There's no way to make your rivals irrelevant while remaining next to them in the same stream. Instead you need to pull away and find new markets. Or, rather, bring your existing market to new customers (and in new ways).

Focus is another component of a successful blue ocean company. Making the shift to blue ocean isn't easy. But for many it is the definition of survival. Focusing gives you an edge by allowing you to trim your fat. But it also gives you clarity from the market's point of view.

Communication, the topic of the next chapter, is the key to applying your value to the market place. It's like the serpentine belt in your car's engine, connecting all the moving parts. Without this, you're creating a lot of energy, but none of the right people are finding out about it.

In the years since 2005, Kim and Mauborgne have been busy helping companies make this shift from the bloody red ocean to the successful blue ocean. In 2017 they released a new book called *Blue Ocean Shift*. While their first book, *Blue Ocean Strategy,* is, as the name implies, a strategy book (and largely about higher concepts), their followup, *Blue Ocean Shift,* provides a more practical look at what it takes to make these changes.

Specifically, *Blue Ocean Shift* highlights a five step process any company can take to make the shift. If you're finding yourself stuck in a me-too market, following these five steps will help you become a market leader, regardless of your size.

Step 1: How to Get Started

Most companies are in the red ocean mindset because, well, most *people* live in the red ocean mindset. It's natural when creating something that will compete for the resources of the market, to peek over the fence at the competition. After all, if they're doing something wrong, that's a cheap lesson for you. And if they're doing something *right*, well then maybe there's a way you can do it better?

But what if this whole approach was the thing that was holding you back? What if this is the very definition of a me-too product, always destined to be positioned as (at very best) an unfortunate second?

When beginning the blue ocean talks with the rest of your team, the first step is to understand the problem (and to make sure that all of the players understand the problem).*

Kim and Mauborgne have created a tool for getting started called the **pioneer-migrator-settler map**. It's a three-stage graph that allows you to evaluate your current market offerings. (See figure 2.1 below)

Pioneer
Value Innovation

Migrator
Value Improvement

Settler
Value Imitation

"Settler" is a product or service that offers incremental changes. Fuel economy that goes from 31 mpg to 32, or a cell phone battery

---

* If you don't have a team, that's okay because the process works the same for individuals.

that lasts 10% longer than the previous version. Everything in this plot is about taking what the market already has and making it better.

"Pioneer," on the other hand, is the opposite. It is a product or service that doesn't already have customers—something new to the market. While these are harder to come up with, this is the area that will both keep your brand fresh and in the lead.

"Migrators" are the middle option, blending the two. They are some of the best products on the market, but they aren't actually innovating (like Pioneers).

(You can download official blue ocean templates, like the Pioneer-Migrator-Settler Map above, as well as other custom templates at fiveroundrocks.com/blue-ocean.)

The very first step has to be understanding exactly what you are providing to the market. *You* love your work. That's why you do it. But is there any objective reason why the market should? Complete the Pioneer-Migrator-Settler Map by plotting each of your offerings as either a pioneer, a migrator, or a settler.

Step 2: Where You are in Relation to the Rest of the Market
Above we looked at divergence and focus as two marks of a blue ocean company. Two examples of this are Southwest Airlines in the 1990s and Cirque du Soleil in the early 2000's. Both companies diverged from their industries and focused their offerings.

In the case of Southwest, they *focused* by getting rid of in-flight meals, airport lounges, and seating choices. And they *diverged* from their competitors with friendly service and speed. Overall, they shifted their philosophy from competing with other airlines, to competing with car-travel. Cirque du Soleil is another example. In the circus market, dominated by Ringling Bros. and Barnum & Bailey, they decided not to compete. They reduced their animal shows as well as the amount of shows offered, and built an entirely new wing focusing on theme, art, and dance. They turned the circus—which was largely entertainment for children—into a place where businesspeople take high-end clients.

Neither Southwest or Cirque du Soleil stumbled upon these direction. They were intentional. And, as Kim and Mauborgne advise, the way to begin this evaluation is through a **strategy canvas**.

A strategy canvas is a grid, where plot both your primary competition, as well as your own offerings. (See figure 2.2 below.)

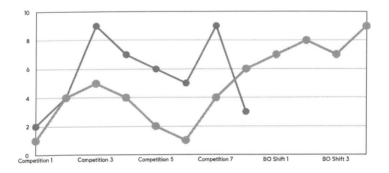

The x axis (horizontal) represents the different attributes of your (and your competition's) offering, while the y axis (vertical) illustrates the range, or impact, of each (high to low). In the case of Southwest, the horizontal axis would include points like meals, lounges, seating choices, friendly service, and speed. Then on the vertical, you plot a point for how well Southwest is doing versus how well their primary competition is doing.

(You can see an example of this along with more instructions at fiveroundrocks.com/resources/blue-ocean.)

Once you've created a strategy canvas, you can not only see how you stack up to your competition, but you've now set the stage to begin seeing *where* you'll create your blue ocean. Again using Southwest, they created a blue ocean by *adding* points to their horizontal axis—points their competition hadn't considered.

Step 3: How to Create Your Best Blue Ocean

This step is all about isolating your customer's pain points. As Kim and Mauborgne note: "In the blue ocean shift process, pain points —which are often hidden—are not constraints. They are blatant opportunities to change the playing field of strategy." This is done through a **buyer utility map**.

Once you understand the *general* truth from your strategy canvas (e.g. "we are a me-too business," or "we can move into abc area by focusing on xyz growth") you can now deepen it with *specifics* of the buyer utility map. This, too, is a grid, where the horizontal axis is the buyer experience cycle, and the vertical axis is the buyer utility levers. (See figure 2.3 below.)

The buyer experience cycle is a six-part sequence that each of your customers will move through: purchase, delivery, use, supplements, maintenance, and disposal. (Note: if you are a service-based organization, the last step, disposal, would function as their transitioning into a newer service—either from you, or *to* you from another provider.)

Alternately, the utility levers are the six variables you can adjust to give your buyers more utility, or benefit. They are customer productivity, simplicity, convenience, risk reduction, fun and

	Purchase	Delivery	Use	Supplements	Maintenance	Disposal
Customer Productivity						
Simplicity						
Convenience						
Risk Reduction						
Fun & Image						
Environmental Friendliness						

image, and environmental friendliness. The more benefit you can add through one of these levers, the more attractive you become to the market.

You use the buyer utility map by putting an O on the areas your industry already focuses on, and you put an X where you've identified a pain point that your industry is not currently focusing on.

The goal here is to have a sparse chart, so you'll want to make sure each O and X is uncontested. If there's any ambiguity or overlap, leave it blank. For more on this, and to download the buyer utility map, visit fiveroundrocks.com/resources/blue-ocean.

Step 4: How to Build Out Step 3
So far, the first three steps have been theoretical. In step four we shift to the practical side.

One of the biggest barriers to creating a blue ocean is not the creating but the *seeing*. Each of us brings our own perspectives and worldviews into everything we do, and the what-has-come-before force brings along with it a particularly strong form of inertia.

Getting people to see differently is often, and quite literally, half of your work. Step four focuses on that by helping you to define a new **value-cost frontier**. In short, this is about looking with fresh eyes at what "value" means to your market, as well as what acceptable costs should be. In other words, it's a rethinking of the basics. (See figure 2.4 below.)

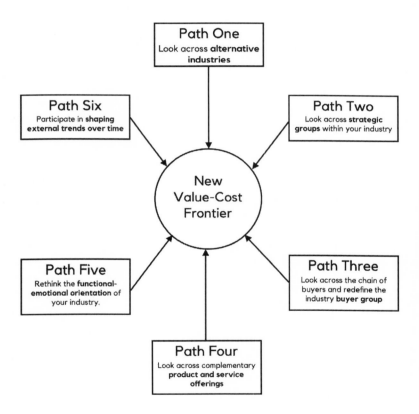

There are six paths to finding this new value-cost frontier. You can take one of them, all of them, or some combination in between. The first path is to look across alternate industries. In the purest sense, this is what your audience is doing. It's like the old saying: no one goes to a hardware store looking for a quarter-inch drill bit. They go looking for a quarter-inch hole. By first looking at alternate industries, you shift your perspective to begin seeing the way your audience does.

The next path is to look across strategic groups *within* your industry. Chick-fil-a did this for the food-service industry by bringing sit-down style service to a fast-food environment. The answers you'll find in this path are often not things that would show up in customer-service surveys. But once your audiences sees them, they are often quick to embrace them.

The third path is to redefine the industry's buyer group. Consider that a sale is often the result of the purchaser, the user, and an influencer—who can often be different people. If your industry typically focuses on, say, the purchaser, what would it look like to market to the user, or the influencer? When cereal brands moved their more colorful cereal to the eye-level of the kids (users), the kids in turn begged mom (the purchaser) to get that kind of cereal at the store.

The fourth path takes a step back and looks at the total solution buyers seek and then asks what complementary products or services help or hurt this total solution? In other words, what is helping (or hurting) your audience when using your product or service? One of Ikea's big markets are young families, but young parents are preoccupied taking care of their kids. So when you go to an Ikea store, you'll also find a daycare.

The fifth path is to rethink the functional-emotional orientation of your industry. If, for instance, you work in a boring industry, what would make it fun? If your industry is intimidating, how can you make it unassuming? People largely buy for emotional reasons, not logical ones, so by addressing this, you'll be able to unlock many buyers who you were otherwise missing.

The sixth path is to look at the macro world around your product. What trends are happening? Can you get in front of them? What if you saw a large trend coming, could you build an infrastructure to be ready for it? The key here is that the trend needs to be large. Small trends reverse as fast as they come. But larger trends have a way of reshaping the market. This works best when you intimately understand the industry you are in.

Step 5: Making the Shift in Your Organization
This final step is about forming the right team to bring your blue ocean strategy to life. In truth, this can often be multiple teams working together. Kim and Mauborgne suggest having a "blue ocean fair," where different teams compete for their ideas to win. The winning is not so much about teams competing against each other, but about teams testing their ideas against each other. For instance, looking at just the six paths from step four, this would create enough for several teams to research and present to the rest. With everyone operating on the same pioneer-migrator-settler map, strategy canvas, and buyer utility map, the group as a whole will be able to see how these new ideas will be received by their audience.

In small organizations a fair might not be necessary. The key benefit of a fair is remaining objective. In larger organization, where departments rarely talk to each other, a fair is almost necessary to break new ground.

Kim and Mauborgne warn of two primary mistakes most teams make. The first is when good ideas get buried in complex language.

When a team falling into this trap presents, it's likely their colleagues won't understand. This is normal. But with some pushback and questions, the concept will begin to emerge. Soon it will be clear if a good idea is there or not. The second problem is that what may seem like a good idea is often nothing more than change for changes's sake. The test here is to ask: is this providing our audience a significant leap in value? If it's not, then there's no actual value here.

Following the fix steps can seem overwhelming, so you can visit my site (fiveroundrocks.com/resources/blue-ocean) to learn more and get resources to begin.

The blue ocean concept is simple: put value where it was previously not. When you do this, the market will respond.

However, the execution—and the hard thinking to get there—is not so simple. This is what keeps most from thinking like this. And for those who do, implementation is never without difficultly. It is for these reasons that many ultimately do not make the shift.

But for those that do, the benefits are plenty. Me-too industries that will popup and copy you will generally take a good 10-15 years to catch up. And once they do, you've already established your position as the leader. It is still necessary to continue innovating, but, by then, the hardest part is certainly past.

highlights

Value is not about creating a good product or service. That's a prerequisite. When it comes to your marketing, value is about *showing* the market you've got something they want.

Before anything else, you need see yourself *objectively*. There is a maxim among photographers that says you are only as good as your last picture. It doesn't matter that you were featured in National Geographic in 1989. What project have you done *this year*? That is what the market is interested in. If you fail to be relevant today, the market will respond accordingly.

Positioning is about making your name first. That may be first to a new market, or first to define a new niche in your current market. Our customers' brains have two categories: one for first, and one for everything else. If you fall into the everything else category, you've lost. What matters most is becoming first in some specific and unique way.

A **blue ocean strategy** is about taking your good value to new markets. Everyone is fighting it out in the red ocean. This is default. And, in a sad way, this is easier. But the most successful companies have differentiated themselves, focused themselves, and learned how to explain both of these unique factors in a way the market appreciates.

chapter three
communication

Everyone is a communicator.

Well, *not really*, but that's a common belief most of us hold. In the cult classic movie, *Office Space*, two consultants ("the Bobs") were brought in to interview employees at a firm and find out who should get fired. In an often quoted scene, Tom Smykowski, an employee of the firm, is feeling the pressure of his interview with the consultants.

Continuing the line of questioning, the first Bob asks, "So what you do is you take the specifications from the customers and you bring them down to the software engineers?"

"That, that's right," says Tom.

"Well, then I gotta ask," says the second Bob, "then why can't the customers just take the specifications directly to the software people, huh?"

"Well, uh" stammers Tom. "Because, uh, engineers are not good at dealing with customers."

"You physically take the specs from the customers?" the first Bob asks, looking over his glasses.

"Well, no, my, my secretary does that…or, or the fax."

"Ah," says the first Bob.

"Then you must physically bring them to the software people," says the second Bob.

"Well…no. Yeah, I mean, sometimes," says Tom.

"Well, what do you say you *do* here?" says the first Bob.

The consultants stare at Tom while he blusters for an answer.

One of the reasons Tom was in a tight spot was because he thought his job was to just show up and not complain too much. He never stopped to consider whether he was providing any value or not.

And the truth is, a lot of businesses look at communication in the same way. As long as they're delivering the facts, then all is well.

But it's not. Far from it.

There's a lot more to solid communication than transmitting data. This chapter looks at those elements as they intersect with your marketing.

your message (and 1,000 others)

For all of our intellectual abilities, and despite our best efforts, we as people don't make logical judgments. We make impulsive ones.

After all, we're busy. We have a lot going on, so we take shortcuts and just do what we did last time.

Think about the last time you made a budget. Like, a full, real budget. My guess is it's been a while (if ever). But, on the face of it, doesn't that seem strange? After all, just about everything in our life depends on cash flow. And a budget is a logical way to manage that.

But in reality, budgets take a lot of energy and time. So what do you do? You keep an eye on your bank account. If it doesn't dip too low, you're doing okay. If it does, you tighten up for a while.

For your audience and their attention, it's the same.

They don't carefully evaluate each and every brand they choose to buy from (or reject), they're much too busy for that. They make quick, snap decisions.

And when your message is competing against hundreds (or, as is often the case, *thousands*) of other messages, you cannot afford to blend in. You cannot afford to wait for your audience to weigh all of the pros and cons before making a decision, because…they won't.

What you need is a faster way—a touchpoint of sorts, that immediately speaks to your audience, telling them, like a Jedi mind trick: *I'm in line with your values. I'm the one you're looking for.*

And while Jedi mind tricks probably only exist in Hollywood, in the world of marketing, there's something that comes pretty close.

It's called storytelling.

Recently storytelling has become a buzzword in business circles. Some of what's out there is good, but a lot of it is just fluff. The main problem is that most books on the subject paint a fuzzy picture, naming the virtues of storytelling, but not actually giving any direction to *how* to do it. Which is a shame, because story is a powerful medium. I regularly speak in front of groups. And without fail, whenever I bring in narrative elements, people sit up and listen. As far back as we can look into recorded history, *story* has been the medium of choice for telling important truths.

And it's no different for businesses today. If you're going to compete in the crowded space that our world has become today, you need to learn to leverage the power of storytelling in your brand.

Briefly, there are two sides to storytelling: the narrative (what we think of as the story itself) and the structural elements, the part that guides the narrative.

In his fascinating book, *Story Engineering*, Larry Brooks, writing to novelists and screenwriters, methodically dissects these elements of story down to the page, explaining what goes where and why it belongs. These are the elements, or beats, of a story. And if you write them wrong, your story will flop.

When it comes to messaging, brands face a similar challenge. There are nonnegotiable elements that if you leave out, your message will get lost in the sea of your competitors' messages.

The good news is, if you tell your story right, your audience will not only hear, but engage.

The other side of story, the narrative, is the essence of what you are saying. It's the part most people think about when we hear 'story.'

But let's put all mechanics aside for a moment. There's something even more important when it comes to telling your story —a point most brands miss. And that is: you're not telling *your* story. You're telling theirs. Your audience's.

Donald Miller's excellent book, *Building a StoryBrand* (which we'll look at in detail later in this chapter), is built on this foundational principle. And in it, he lays out the seven steps for how do build a story into your brand that causes customers to listen.

This kind of thinking is vital because most in your audience will only give you a few seconds before they move on. When we see hundreds of ads, and receive thousands of messages (all in a single day), our filters for what to give our attention to has to be pretty high.

Story (if done right) is the tool that will help us break through that filter.

In fact it may be one of the only tools that consistently works.

why your brain likes story so much

Through the ages, story was used to pass down important truths from older generations. Today we have books and google for that. But story is no less important. And the reason is because of *why* story works.

The reason story was used as a communication tool in the past —and why it is still one of the most powerful tools today—is because it taps into the part of our brain that makes decisions: our emotions.

"When an emotion is triggered in your brain," writes psychologist, Mary Lamia. "Your nervous system responds by creating feelings in your body (what many people refer to as a 'gut feeling') and certain thoughts in your mind."

In other words, emotions are what tell us how to think about —or how to judge—a situation. They connect what's happening in the world with the value system we hold to.

It is from this point that we organize our lives, decide what our futures should hold, and take the steps necessary to get there.

Neurologist Antonio Damasio tells the story of one of his patients, Eliot, who had surgery on his brain to remove a tumor. Before the surgery Eliot was a successful businessman. He was incredibly smart, testing in the top 97th percentile for IQ. And, fortunately, after the surgery, his intellect was still in tact.

However, post-surgery, other things were different. He could no longer make decisions. He could tell you answers, but he couldn't make judgments about which of those answers were better. Before the surgery he was a leading manager in his career and held an influential place in his community. After the surgery, he couldn't keep his job, he was taken by a con man, and ultimately, divorced from his wife.

What happened during the surgery? The tumor was located in his prefrontal cortex, and so, as a result, a small part of Elliot's brain was removed. While Elliot himself was still healthy, he was notably different post-surgery. Researchers have learned from cases like Elliot and others that the prefrontal cortex is one of the areas responsible for controlling emotions.

Without the ability to control his emotions, he could not make judgments.

As Lisa Cron, writing in her book *Wired for Story*, puts it: "he was utterly detached and approached life as if everything in it was neutral." Because "without emotion, each option carried the exact same weight."

This holds an important lesson for communicators: if we're not tapping into the emotions of our listeners, we're not going to be very effective at moving them to act.

But how do you reach a person's emotions? Especially a person who you may not have even met?

The answer is that you have to bypass the 'rational' filter that will come up with reasons to ignore or reject you, and you have to interact with the emotional/judgment side directly. In other words, we need to bypass the thinking, conscious side of audience's minds and jump straight to the emotional, subconscious side.

Noble prize winner and psychologist Daniel Kahneman calls these two sides of our mind System 1 and System 2.

System 1 is automatic and "fast." Our subconscious. System 2 is slower and more deliberate. It's our analytical self. When we react instinctively, it's System 1 in our brain that's making the call. When we stop and think through a situation, we're engaging in System 2-thinking.

Most of us think of ourselves as "System 2" people. After all, we're not rash. We make informed decisions. But the truth is, that kind of thinking takes a lot of work. Our brains operate by trying to *conserve* calories, and System 2-thinking does just the opposite. Think about sitting down to do the equivalent of long division every time you want to do, well, *anything*. That would be utterly exhausting.

And that's where System 1 comes in.

Through a series of **heuristics** (patterns, or *stories,* in which we categorize our world), we're able to use the wisdom of our System 2, without burning the resources it normally takes. Think of it like Google. Somebody had to put all that stuff in there and create the algorithms so that we could find it again. But once it's done, it's super easy to use. Just type in a few key words and and click search. That's how System 1 and System 2 work. System 2 is the hard mental work of our brains learning new things. System 1 is the short-cut of accessing that previous learning.

So what does all of this have to do with story? When we hear stories, the emotions (judgment) centers of our brains are activated and we largely shift to autopilot. And if we hear the right *kind* of story (more on that in the next section), not only are we in tune with the message, but we *automatically* accept it.

That, in a nutshell, is the power of story.

It does what logical arguments cannot: it jumps the fence of our subconscious and taps into our deeper identities and aspirations.

And so when a potential customer sees or hears from you, they will immediately (and subconsciously) make a judgment, based on a feeling, about your message. In an instant, they will categorize it as either something to help them, or something to discard and move on.

Fortunately, story gives us the time-tested formula for organizing our message in a way that will be received.

But not all stories are created equal. And not by a long shot.

There are rules to effective storytelling. These rules, or elements, are to where we now turn.

how to tell your brand's story

A story is *not* a narrative or recounting of past event, it's a *framework*.

And because it's a framework, like any other structure, there are rules. The facts of the story can be true or false, but if you miss the framework, you miss the chance to connect.

Donald Miller's company StoryBrand teaches brands how to tell their story in a way that is clear and cuts through the noise of the thousands of other daily messages your audience will hear. Through the years he's narrowed it down to seven components, which he describes in a single sentence:

The character has a problem and meets a guide, who gives them a plan and calls them to action, that helps them avoid failure and ends in success.

If you filter your message through the seven components captured in the above sentence, you'll find your audience not only responds to your message, but *identifies* with it. And ultimately, they'll choose you not because you have the best product (you may or may not), but because you have the *clearest message*.

People buy what they understand—what they perceive to be valuable. And running your message through story principles is about doing exactly that.

Here is the seven-part framework:

1. The Character

Most brands start with themselves. After all, it's *their* bottom line that, at the end of the day, they need to be watching. In a lot of ways, this is perfectly normal. Each morning, *you* get up, go to *your* job, and move about accomplishing *your* tasks. Seeing things through our own lens is both natural and heathy.

Healthy, that is, for us as individuals.

But not healthy for us as brands.

What successful brands know is that they are not the focal point (or hero) in their story. Their customer is. When Coke creates an ad, they do not ask their customers to buy a coke, and they don't talk about the wonders of Coke. They instead show happy and fulfilled people enjoying a coke. The ad is not about

Coke—it's about their customers, because Coke understands very well that their customers are the hero in the story.

Making this shift starts with narrowing down your audience's desire. What are they looking for? What are they trying to become? Your story begins where *their* story begins.

2. Has a Problem

Without a problem, there is no story. Without some risk of loss or a longing for more, there is no *need*. And without need, what are we here for?

This point works in tandem with the first. By understanding your character you are working to understand their problem.

Miller breaks the customer problem down into three distinct categories.

First, there is an "external" problem. This is what is physically or obviously blocking them for engaging with you.

I live in New Orleans. And while my house has never flooded, it's located in an area that requires flood insurance. The other day FEMA (the Federal Emergency Management Agency responsible for natural disasters*) sent me a letter saying I needed a new elevation certificate, or my flood insurance (something they regulate directly) would start climbing at a rate of up to *18% per year*.

My external problem: I need an elevation certificate.

---

* If you lived in New Orleans during Hurricane Katrina, your opinion of FEMA is decidedly low. There were, many argue, not much they could have done worse during that time. My editor—a fellow New Orleans—thought I probably meant to write "responsible for responding to natural disasters" instead of "responsible for" and suggested I change it. I compromised with a footnote.

So I googled it, found a company, and set an appointment.

But during my search, I didn't go for the first company I found. I looked around and found one that seemed competent, had a good price, and would give me an elevation certificate FEMA wouldn't balk at.

The reason is because, despite my external problem, I was actually *buying* based on the second category of problem: my "internal" problem.

The internal problem, simply, is how you *feel* about the external problem. The two work together. Our audience is searching for a solution to their external problem but buying based on their internal problem.

My concern was to quickly resolve this potential 18%-per-year rate hike. That means I needed someone who knew what FEMA wanted, and I needed them to do it at a reasonable price. Internally, I was *anxious* to avoid paying a big unnecessary bill.

In the end, I didn't go with a company that could simply give me an elevation certificate (my external problem), I went with one that assuaged my fears (my internal problem). And this is the same way your customers buy.

But there's also a third level of problem. It's called the "philosophical" problem. And understanding this allows you to best *communicate* your customer's problem. Think of it in terms of "should" or "ought."

I'll use my FEMA example again. As a responsible home-owner, I *shouldn't* need to worry about being blind-sided by rate hikes outside of my control. I *ought* to be able to focus on more important things: providing for my family and focusing my energy on them.

When you talk to your audience in terms of their philosophical problem, you begin to create movement. You see their heads nodding in agreement. You are telling them: I am not here to take advantage of your situation—I am here because I believe you *shouldn't* be in this situation at all. Using philosophical language taps into the core beliefs of your audience. And when you speak this language to them, you communicate that you really do understand their problem.

When it comes to your audience's problem, you begin by clearly outlining the external, then you *sell* the internal, and finally, you *speak to* the philosophical.

When you talk in terms of your hero's problem, you create relevance. And when you put them as the hero in the story, you capture their attention. But that leaves the question: if your customer is the hero, then what role do *you* play in all of this?

3. Meets a Guide

You are the guide, their Dumbledore or Gandalf. You are powerful, and accomplished, and confident, and you are there *to serve them*. This is the purpose of the guide.

Once you begin to see your audience as the hero, your mission and work naturally becomes about their problem.

The guide is an important (but peripheral) character. She is always in the story, but the story is never *about* her. When all a brand does is talk about themselves—how great they are, their history—what are they communicating? That they are the guide, or that they are the hero? Simply put, talking about yourself puts you —not your audience—in the position of the hero.

The problem with playing the role of the hero is one of competition. When you step into the hero role you are now *competing* with your customer for the spotlight. At least, in their subconscious you are. They didn't wake up this morning wondering how they could make *your* life better. Their day is about *them*.

You step into the role of guide by showing authority. There are two ways you can do this: by connecting your name to other names your audience already trusts (testimonials or other authorities), and by displaying empathy.

If you are a small business marketing to other businesses, then you may tactfully display the symbols of universally trusted brands who've trusted you in the past. And when appropriate, you'll use testimonials, showing your audience others, like them, who have experienced success from working with you. In short, authority is anything that tells your audience: "You can trust me, because these people who you already trust, or who are just like you, have also trusted me."

The other half to speaking guide language is empathy. By telling your audience that you not only understand their pain, but that you've been there and felt their pain, you establish immediate rapport.

There is a lot of latitude in these two components. Through empathy you can speak to your qualifications. And through testimonials or other authorities, you can illustrate your portfolio and past wins.

4. Gives them a Plan

A good guide has their stuff together. Your plan is where you tell your audience how to get started.

Giving your audience a plan is about confidence (their opinion of you) and simplicity (your path for them). When you provide a coherent plan, everything they've heard so far is confirmed. You *are* the guide they need. And when you provide a plan that is simple, you stand out like a light on a hill in an otherwise busy, noisy world. In the market today, simplicity is the divider that separates you from your competition.

When it comes to crafting the plan, the most effective plans are between three or four steps. If your process is more than three or four steps, it's best to condense it to the three or four *big* steps. There's no need to give them every detail, you simply need to show them the map. Giving them the big points will help them mentally frame how the process will look.

But if you're on the other end of this, and the process to get started working with you is really only one step ("buy my widget"), you still frame it in three steps. Three is a powerful number. It is not too simple, but not too complex. It is complete. And so by bringing your one step up to three, you fill your audience's subconscious need to see a complete plan. It may be something as simple as: (1) Check out the features of our widget, (2) click here to buy it, and then (3) start experiencing widget success in your life.

By offering a clear plan, you take away another obstacle. Slowly, you are making doing business with you seem to be the most reasonable decision.

5. *Calls them to Action*

This is the clear finish line.

Your call to action may be included in one of your steps above ("buy now") or it may not. But what needs to be clear in the minds of your audience is that *this* is your expectation for them.

This really goes back to simplicity. When your audience doesn't know what you want them to do, two things happen. They lose interest, because they're not sure what exactly you're about. And second—and perhaps most obviously—*they don't do the thing you want them to do.*

For instance, if you're a nonprofit or a church, what's the number one thing you want them to do? (Hint: it's not *your* number one need, which is usually "give now.") Most likely the number one thing you want them to do is connect. Connect with either you, or to others already connected with you. Because once they've done this, they'll be bought-in to what you stand for. And from there they'll be much more willing to support you (the "give now").

The call to action needs to be extremely clear. In my example above, if your call to action is for your audience to connect, you need to be explicit on what exactly "connecting" is. Something like: "Join our next community gathering" or "Visit a service this week" are examples of explicit calls to action.

Some leaders are concerned that this level of directness will turn off their audience. But it doesn't. In fact, it *never* does. If, perhaps, you were the only brand in the entire world, then *maybe* that level of directness could be a turn off. But you're not the only brand. In fact, you're only a tiny sliver of their world. And they're only going to give you a few seconds of their time before moving on. So your call to action needs to be crystal clear.

6. Helps them Avoid Failure

Failure is like salt. Without it, there's not much taste. But with too much of it, your food is no longer edible. When using salt, you need to use just enough. And so it is with failure: you need to use it, but not too much of it.

Bringing failure into your communication works because failure puts *stakes* in the game. If you don't show your audience what their world would look like without using your product or service, then why should they bother with it?

But if all you ever do is talk about how they could fail, they're going to go somewhere else, because, well, your message is depressing.

Use failure, but use it sparingly.

7. And Ends in Success

Finally, the promised land.

In case you haven't figured it out yet: you were *never* selling your product or service. You're selling a success. Your product just happens to be the key to your audience finding their success.

At some point in your message, you need to give your audience a picture of what you're really promoting: a better life for your audience. If you're honest and create good work, then that's all you want for them anyway. Letting them know this reminds them that you and your work really is a good fit for them.

These seven steps are not about telling a story—not in the sense the word usually evokes. Instead, this is about using the *principles* of story to communicate your message effectively.

As I've worked with clients, helping them apply these same principles, I've seen the same thing over and over again: a flood of relief and excitement as we've walked through this process. So many of my clients know exactly what they do, but they've always struggled with getting *their* audience to understand.

By taking your message through these seven steps you'll not only be able to clearly communicate your brand, but you'll be able to cut through the noise your audience is bombarded with and speak directly to their needs.

how to write words people want to read

> No matter how beautiful your website is. No matter how
> exceptional your guarantee is. No matter how much you care.
> If you're the same as everyone else, you're doomed.
> - RAMIT SETHI, entrepreneur, author

The essence of your marketing is your words.

This may seem like an overstatement to some. But it's true. It's not your design—though that is important. It's not the functionality of your website—though that too can make a big difference. It's simply the words you use to communicate.

The reason words are so important is that they are the least ambiguous tool you have. Words are the clearest way to communicate to your audience.

And the reason *written* words are so relevant is because of scale. You will meet most of your audience through some non-direct channel, like your website, an ad, social media, or your product itself. And so how you represent yourself there is how they will experience you.

But you don't have to be a "writer" to get this right. Good writers are certainly valuable. But when it comes to your written marketing, what's more important than being a good writer is being a good *communicator*. That is, understanding the message that needs to be communicated.

This process is called **copywriting**.

Copywriting has the single goal of converting. That's it. Some highly effective (and highly paid) copywriters are not even that good at grammar and spelling. (For the record, I do suggest you have someone proof read your stuff before you publish it to the world. My point here is that polish is not what actually sells.) But they understand what people need to read (or hear) and when those parts need to happen.

In his book, *How to Write Copy that Sells*, Ray Edwards—a master copywriter himself—outlines four critical elements of being a great copywriter.

As soon as you begin to think like this, you're on your way to becoming a copywriter. And that means your marketing just became instantly more effective.

1. Get Your Headlines Right

People skim.

Unfortunately for us marketers, when it comes to text on website or marketing emails, our audience isn't reading every word. Most will only give you a quick glance, and so you need something that will hook them.

One of the best tools in your arsenal is your headline. Headlines are what grab your readers' attention. Brian Clark, the founder of copyblogger.com, notes that "on average, 8 out of 10 people will read a headline, but only 2 out of 10 will go on to read the content."

This, of course, is not an excuse to cut corners in what you put *under* the headlines. In fact, when people skim headlines, they're looking for points of interest where they'll jump in and read in detail.

There are three common mistakes writers and marketers will make here. First, their headlines will be cute instead of clear. This may be fun from the perspective of the writer, but for the reader, it doesn't work. You need a solid and familiar relationship before this will work. And even then you have to be careful. If you're toying with cute, resist and focus on *clear* instead.

Second, and much like the first, the headlines are often clever instead of clear. Clever requires thinking on the part of our audience. In our busy world, it is a very small group that will stop and take the time to decipher your message. Most will pass on it before they realize there is benefit for them.

The third kind of ineffective headlines is one that forgets to offer the reader a promise. Why should I swap my time and energy

—two limited resources—to invest in what you've just written? What's in it for me? If the answers to these questions are not clearly laid out in your headline, then your writing will likely fall into the 80% that doesn't get read.

It is the job of the headline to *clearly* lay out the promise of reading. Without this, whatever great insights or solutions you've included will be buried and overlooked. Good, compelling writing starts with a strong headline.

2. Use Bullet points

Did I mention people skim?

Bullet points are like speed bumps. They're easy to spot. And they're even easier to read. When you break up your copy with bullet points, your reader's eye finds these lines and reads them like a summary of value. It's as if their brain sees them and automatically asks, "Is there anything here I'm missing and should go back and catch?"

In effect, bullet points become the second half of a one-two punch you started with a good headline. If you have good bullet points, you're whetting the appetite of your reader so that they'll dig into your copy. The longer they spend with you (and your copy) the more familiar they become—which means, the greater the chance of buying.

What makes a good bullet point? They highlight relevant features. It may be a reward or a payoff or an outline of the reader's problem. Anything that speaks meaningfully to your reader works here.

But the key is they must be relevant. Bullet points are not just a formatting for listing information. They are like a flag or beacon in the middle of your copy calling readers to slow down and investigate. They need to be talking to exactly what your listener is trying to avoid (or, conversely, who they are trying to become).

3. State the problem (and then amplify it)

Out of the gate, you need to state the problem. But then you need to amplify it.

How do you do this? By spelling out the implications of the problem.

In his groundbreaking work on major sales (something more expensive than an impulse buy), researcher Neil Rackham found that successful sales people always did this. It's not enough to state the problem. You have to *work out* the implications of the problem for your audience.

Successful sellers "take a problem that the buyer perceives to be small," writes Rackham, "and build it up into a problem large enough to justify action."

At this point, some begin to feel uneasy. "I don't want to *trick* my audience." And you shouldn't. But if you've taken the time to create this good work, it's because you believe it's worth the investment. In the building and preparing process, you became (if you weren't already) convinced of the need. *You're* already a believer.

But your customers aren't.

They haven't seen what you've seen. They're still bombarded by the thousands of other offers and pitches for their time. So when you amplify the problem, you're not manipulating them—you're helping them understand what you've long known: this is worth their time (or energy or money).

4. Make a guarantee (really)

The customer journey is difficult. You need to take as many obstacles and distractions out of the way as possible.

One important obstacle is the risk of being a sucker. That might come in the form of losing money, wasting time, or missing an opportunity—that is, whatever real or imagined risk that comes along with them buying from you.

When you offer a real and meaningful guarantee—you're telling them, I trust my product so much, that if for some strange reason you don't like it, it is valuable enough to me to take back.

But do guarantees really work? I mean, doesn't *everything* have a guarantee on it?

Yes and no. Yes, they still work. There's a reason why infomercials still always have a guarantee. As cheesy as they seem, infomercials are still a highly lucrative marketing channel.

But a guarantee looses its power when it's too common or generic. If you're selling red radios and tell your customer: "If you're not happy in 30 days, bring it back." Well, of course. Isn't that pretty much the standard everywhere? But if you told them: "If you're not happy in *three-hundred* and thirty days, you can still bring it back," then that's a special guarantee. Or, if you're selling new cars, what happens the minute it drives off the lot? It looses 20-30% of its value. What if your guarantee told customers they could drive it around for a week (or a month), and if they didn't like it, you'd give them 100% of its value back, including fees and taxes?

The idea behind a guarantee is that it removes risk.

But a guarantee is a good opportunity to not only decrease risk but to *increase* value. In Seth Goden's book *Free Prize Inside!* he talks about including something extra that is also remarkable. When you do this, people will tell their friends, and your stuff will stand out.

Pulling all of this together, copywriting is about presentation. There are a certain set of problems that your audience has. And they're looking for a specific solution—even one they might not yet know about.

Copywriting is about effectively speaking to—and answering —that need.

how to start: part one

Getting started writing your copy can be difficult. Many times our instinct is to start at the beginning. *Why am I here? What is the purpose of all of this?* And this is a natural starting place. It is, after all, *the beginning.*

The problem is: it's boring.

And boring things get ignored.

Your marketing is competing with thousands of other messages, and, likely, millions of other stimuli. The truth is, no one is going to stick around if you don't show them results *immediately.*

The backstory, or the *why,* is still important because it's what brought you to this place. But it's not the payoff. Your audience isn't interested in that. They want the meat: *how do I answer my question now?*

Screen writers and novelists have long understood this. And they have a solution. It's called *in medias res.* This is a Latin phrase for starting in the middle of the action.

Perhaps one of the greatest examples of this is Homer's 2,700 year old story, *The Odyssey*. The story picks up with Odysseus' journey (the entire narrative) almost completely behind him. The reader learns the story through flashbacks and recollections. In this way, there are two points of reference: the end—which is where we started—and the beginning, or middle—the flashback moments. Throughout the book, the reader is anticipating how the two will align.

Martin Scocese's *Raging Bull* (1980) is another, more recent example. It's the true story of acclaimed boxer, Jake LaMotta (played by Robert De Niro). LaMotta had an impressive career, including a match where he beat Sugar Ray Robinson—a man considered by many to be one of the greatest boxers.

But the movie doesn't begin here. It opens with LaMotta preparing to perform a stand-up comedy show. Throughout the movie, we see LaMotta's rise and fall. We see how he went from international acclaim to lonely and now preparing to do a comedy routine.

How does using *in medias res* instantly hook your audience? By immediately giving them what they came for: the action. And when you start to look for it, you'll see this all the time in books and movies.

This translates to your marketing when you can focus on what your audience is *most* interested in. What is the primary pain point of your audience? Or what are they trying to become above all else? *This* is your starting point.

But there's an important caveat to *in medias res*. Beginning in the middle of the action does not mean you start with your resolution. If you do, there's no problem to amplify, or itch to scratch. *In medias res* is not about beginning with the answer, it's about beginning with your audience's biggest problem. In other words, it's the part *just before* the answer.

Think back to *Raging Bull*. Why is this world-renowned boxer preparing to do stand-up comedy? What happened to all of his fame? Is there some twist? Do we not have the full story? The same principles that work so well in story are what fuel your marketing. By starting at the height of the problem, you become acutely relevant to your audience. In effect, you are priming them to desire your solution. And that is why *in medias res* works.

If you're selling little red wagons, you don't sell the toy. Instead, you sell the desire. The nostalgia. The father-son bonding time. Or the ability for a dad to re-live his childhood memories and to now pass them on to his boy.

In marketing, *in medias res* jumps straight to what is most important.

how to start: part two

In medias res is only the first half of your start. It's where you go next that determines the effectiveness of your start.

To use an old metaphor: it doesn't matter how attractive your bait is. If you don't have a solid line, the fish still gets away. It's the bait and the line together that catches the fish. And so now we look at that second part, the line.

About a hundred years ago, a young, unknown psychologist discovered something that has since generated over 600 studies confirming its results. Bluma Zeigarnik and her mentor, the famous psychologist, Kurt Lewin, were eating at a restaurant one day when Zeigarnik noticed how her waiter flawlessly remembered their order, every single time. She wondered if he had exceptional memory, or if it was something else.

So she did an experiment. She asked everyone at her table to cover their plates, and then she asked the waiter to come back and tell them, for memory, what he'd delivered only seconds earlier.

But he could only remember about half of what he'd just delivered.

A moment ago he'd remembered everyone's order perfectly. But now, when asked to remember again, he couldn't. What was going on?

From this and other experiments like it, Zeigarnik went on to discover what's now known as the Zeigarnik Effect: our brains give heightened attention to incomplete tasks while largely ignoring the completed ones.

So as long as the waiter's order was incomplete, his mind kept it front and center. But as soon as the food had been delivered, that information was wiped clean and almost completely forgotten.

As marketers, this has a massive impact on how we communicate. If we want our audience to engage, then we have to present our information in a way that causes them to naturally do just that. And we do this by creating an open loop in their mind.

By creating an open loop (or, story loop), we create an unresolved issue—one that needs to be solved. Think about the black and white movie that opens with the girl tied to the train tracks while we hear the whistle and puffing in the distance. Or, one of my personal favorites: The opening scene of Raiders of the Lost Ark, where Indy is walking through the jungle when they spot a poison dart in a tree—then the camera pulls back to reveal one of his own men has pulled a gun on him in an attempt to shoot him in the back.

When we see scenes like this, we want to know more. Why is this happening? What other information am I missing? By opening a story loop we tap into our audience's want for resolution.

In marketing, a story loop isn't too different from a movie. Your client has a problem. Starting right there (*in medias res*) and then leaving it *temporarily* without an answer helps heighten the need for resolution.

A classic example of this is an ad that begins with the words: "I light cigarettes, cigars, pipes, candles, lamps, fires, stoves, fridges, geysers, Christmas puddings and distress flares and I cost three hundredths of a cent."

The list is eclectic enough. But the last line ("and I cost three hundredths of a cent") throws the story loop wide open. What, if anything, only costs three hundredths of a cent? And how could it be involved with that list of things?

As you look down, you see the words: "It's easy to see I'm not in it for the money," next to a picture of a match.

This is from a classic ad for Lion Matches. Everyone knows what matches do. That part is obvious. And the match itself is pretty simple and boring. But by opening a story loop, these copywriters turn the mundane into the interesting.

Communicating is all about attention. Elmore Leonard, the author of *Get Shorty*, once gave this advice to writers: "When you write, try to leave out all the parts that readers skip." His point is why *in medias res* and opening story loops work: The action and intrigue are what people are interested in. And the more you give it to them, the more they'll pay attention to you.

highlights

In marketing, communication is the systematic telling of your story.

Our tendency, once we've spent a lot of time on our work, is to see it disproportionately. To see a bit more than it is. In truth, there is a ton of other comparable work in the market. The way we cut through this is by tapping into the judgment centers of our audience's brains and leveraging the elements of **story**.

Emotions are our gateway into story. Emotions are the judgment centers in our brains, and they are the reasons we make decisions. For our stories to be effective, they must tap into this emotional center.

But stories are more than emotion. There is a structure we must follow, because it holds certain keys that our audience is listening for. We must step into the role of a guide, understand their pain points, offer a clear plan, and speak to their aspirational identities.

Copywriting is a specifically valuable skill for applying storytelling. Headlines—perhaps the most important part—are what grab our audience's attention the fastest. Following this, the use of bullet points, problem amplification, and other language will help you speak the right message in the right way.

The best place to begin, for both you as a creator, but also your listeners, is right in the middle. This is an age-old technique called *in medias res*. By starting with what's interesting, and then opening a story loop, you immediately hook your audience's attention.

direction

O nce you've focused your message, built in overwhelming value, and even honed your communication into its most effective form, there is still one more key strategy you'll need to incorporate. It answers the question: how do you specifically direct your message? More than anything else, this chapter looks at the packaging and context with which your marketing will flow.

The "packaging" here is not the literal box or bag your widget comes in, but the social influence that guides your audience to *want* it.

Marketing that does not consider how an audience is influenced or how individuals make decisions, is marketing hinged mostly on luck. The first three strategies of this book are vital. But in many ways the concepts there seem obvious: focus, show your value, and communicate effectively.

But this final strategy is different. Here we will look at the hidden forces of influence that are guiding our audience to (or away from) us.

the fallacy of logic

Logic doesn't win arguments.

Take a look at politics. Or cigarette smoking. Or the entire fast-food industry. If we were persuaded by logic, politics wouldn't be the circus it is, cigarette smoking would be nonexistent, and we wouldn't even recognize the fast-food industry.

But instead, year after year, these things stay the same.

The reason harkens back to a point from the last chapter: people do not make decisions based on logic, they make them based on emotions.

In a now classic study, psychologist Ellen Langer showed that logic does in fact play a role, but often not the one we think. Back in the days before computers, where offices shared a single Xerox copying machine, the lines to make a copy were often long. In her experiment, Langer had people walk to the front and ask: "Excuse me, I have 5 pages. May I use the Xerox machine?"

Her results: a pleasant 60% of the time, members in the line would let the undercover experimenter cut.

But then she tweaked it slightly. She added a bit of logic, a "because" statement. This time her testers again asked to cut, but they added an irrelevant "because" to the request: "Excuse me, I have 5 pages. May I use the Xerox machine, because I have to make copies?"

Her results were a stunning *93%* success rate.

Due simply to an arbitrary "because" tacked on to the end of the request, people were inclined to let someone go before them over 50% more than without the "because."

What is just as fascinating is that she did another version of this experiment where she changed the "because" to something relevant ("because I'm in a rush"). Her results were 94% success. In other words, it made almost no difference about the content of her "because" statement, *as long as it was present*.

In essence, logic is very much like this. What Langer showed is that people often do not *interact* with the logic presented to them. They merely look for signs that it is present (the "because" statement in the above example). But rarely will they interact with the logic (Such as: "So what if you have papers—you wouldn't be in this line if you didn't! That's no reason to cut.").

We see this a lot in everyday life, too. Think back to the discussion of categories from chapter one. When we visit a doctor's office, we don't first examine her med school records or google any potential malpractice suits she's been involved in. We just show up, and if she has a waiting room, is wearing a white coat, and takes our insurance without any problem, then we're good. She meets the most common qualities of the "doctor" category, and at that point, our brain quits asking questions.

If statistically there is little difference between, a logical "because" and an illogical one, does this mean we should build a bunch of irrelevant "because" statements into our marketing? Definitely not. At the very least, doing this—especially online or in print—is a receipt for that small minority who does pay attention to find you and call you out.

But it also doesn't work for another reason: you *want* people to interact with your logic. Your logic is the force of your marketing. It's what comprises your focus and value and communication. If people are not actually engaging with that, then what is separating you from the rest of the noise?

So what do we do? How do we overcome the fact that most people expect logic but few will engage with it?

The answer is in **rhetoric.**

In his superb book, *Thank You for Arguing*, Jay Heinrichs defines rhetoric as "the art of persuasion" and deals primarily with the "advantageous" kind that is "what's best for an audience, community, or nation."

The value of rhetoric is that it jolts an otherwise unfocused audience into paying attention. While rhetoric mostly takes the form of spoken words, the same concepts can be applied to written works.

Heinrich outlines seven techniques to use rhetoric effectively:

First, rearrange your words. You can do this by twisting a tired cliché or change a common word order. Another form of this is editing out loud—purposefully backing mid-sentence and changing what you previously said. You can also adjust your speaking volume (up or down), or invent new words. These are all methods that will cause your audience to pay closer attention to what you're actually saying.

Second, use your audience's code. By using language exclusive to your group, you build trust. A corollary to this is to use words *opposite* of what your opponent or competition is using. If you repeat what your competition is saying, you will be seen as being a different version of the same thing. As we saw in chapter two, your vocabulary is in line with moving from blue ocean to red ocean.

Third, form (or tap into) an identity for the group. Heinrichs writes, "the surest way to commit an audience to an action is to get them to identify with it—to see the choice as one that helps define them as a group." The more your language reflects your audience, the more they will be interested, and persuaded, by what you have to say.

Fourth, lead your audience. By getting your audience to describe themselves, in their own words, one of the first things to appear is "*their* best sense of who they are." Next, your job is to say that back to them and *direct* them to a place consistent with that identity. Politics aside, in the 2016 campaign Donald Trump did an excellent job of using his audience's words back to them. (He also did this by wearing a red trucker hat.)

Fifth, avoid apologizing. To some this may seem unethical. And in some instances, it might not be at all appropriate. However, the essence of this fifth technique is to *frame* your error in a way that keeps you (in the mind of your audience) as the leader. Heinrichs recommends practical points like: be the first to break the news, switch immediately to the (hopeful) future, avoid belittling the victim, and instead of apologizing, "express your feelings about not living up to your standards." The difference between this and completely not apologizing is the focus. The latter gets stuck on your incompetence, while the former empathizes with the pain your error caused.

Sixth, use the occasion's specifics. Time and place can have a big impact on how your audience receives your message. This is similar to the concept of positioning discussed in chapter two. Pay attention to and use the specific elements of the place where your audience will hear your message. If you're outdoors, in a small indoor room, or near something of historical significance, these are all primers for your message.

Seventh, use the right medium. While the sixth is about the point of reception, the seventh is about the medium that gets it there. This includes, if you're giving a live address, your body language. And—depending on your product or service—if you can incorporate smell, taste, and touch, these are senses highly susceptible to emotional factors.

Much more can be said about all of these. But for the purpose of your marketing, the power of rhetoric is the ability to shape your message.

Contrary to the hint of the title, none of this needs to be *illogical*. Logic, in fact, is often the base with which each of these points rests. However, what we've looked at here is *presentation*. To present in a purely logical fashion—without appealing to emotion and other relevant factors—is almost always the weaker option.

no need to think

In the last chapter, we looked at System 1 and System 2 of our brain and the concept of heuristics. If you recall, System 1 is much like our subconscious while System 2 is our conscious. **Heuristics**, on the other hand, is the shortcut System 1 takes, based on what it's learned from System 2.

Heuristics comes in to play regularly in our daily lives. When we drive a certain way to work every morning, we're assuming it's the fastest or most efficient route when in fact it might just be the most familiar. We regularly buy the same brands, even when others are better, though that decision may just be a result of repeated exposure. And we invoke "common sense" by giving a snap judgment on a matter we haven't actually considered.

However, in each of these cases—and many others like them—the explanations we give for our decisions are often not the real reasons we do them. In other words, they are the reasons we *give* them, not the reasons that went into our decision making process.

So why *do* what we do?

The answer is the result of three factors, often working together: familiarity, anchors, and less-is-more. Familiarity breads trust, the more often we see something, the more we subconsciously begin to trust it. Anchors provide a standard. This is our starting point for adjusting up or down. And the notion that less is more satisfies our System 1's heuristic bias of doing easy work over hard.

Factor 1: Familiarity

The "maintenance required" light on my dashboard in my car came on a few months back. At first it concerned me. And as soon as it came on, I couldn't help thinking about it every time I got in my car. *I just had my oil changed. They probably forgot to reset it. There's a weird way to reset it. I'll need to do that.* But soon my thinking switched to: *What if it's not that? What if something big is wrong? What if I have to take my car into the shop? That's going to be a pain...*

Now, even as I write this, the light is still on, but I'm not bothered by it anymore. Well—a small part of my brain is. But for the most part, I've automatically switched to ignoring it. I still see it, of course, but it just doesn't bother me anymore. I've grown accustomed to it.

Cognitive psychologist Larry Jacoby explains that "the experience of familiarity has a simple but powerful quality of 'pastness' that seems to indicate that it is a direct reflection of prior experience." So by seeing that little light on my dash, day after day, my brain has shifted it from the current need-to-address-today problem to the equivalent of a *past* event.

This is why procrastination seems to have such a compounding effect. Because, in our minds, *it does*. Every day you are reminded of a task but put it off, your brain sees it as more and more of a past event, instead of a current pending one.

So what happens when we take this phenomenon and apply it to our marketing? We're able to build *trust*.

By using the same logo, brand colors, and even *words* in our communication, we are building the neural pathways for our audience. As psychologist and Nobel prize winner, Daniel Kahneman, writes: "Words that you have seen before become easier to see again—you can identify them better than other words when they are shown very briefly or masked by noise, and you will be quicker (by a few hundredths of a second) to read them than to read other words. In short, you experience greater cognitive ease in perceiving a word you have seen earlier, and it is this sense of ease that gives you the impression of familiarity."

But it's more than cognitive ease. Kahneman continues: "the familiarity of one phrase in the statement sufficed to make the whole statement feel familiar, and therefore true."

This is pretty amazing. By using repetition, our brains begin to trust. And because of our associative nature, those same (now) trustworthy words and images extend to the rest of what we do.

Psychologist Robert Zajonc once did an experiment in the school papers for the University of Michigan and Michigan State by simply putting a small ad-like box on the front page with nothing but a few Turkish looking works. Words like *kadirga* and *saricik* and *biwonjni*. The "ad" ran for several weeks. Some words were used often, and some were used less. But no explanation was ever given for why it was there.

Later a survey was sent out to the students and they were asked to rate the words in the ad. Do you believe they mean something good? Or something bad? the questionnaire asked. The results? "The words that were presented more frequently were rated much more favorably than the words that had been shown only once or twice."

This is a phenomenon Zajonc has dubbed the ***mere exposure effect***. By simply exposing the students to them, their trustworthiness *increased* based on how often they were exposed.

And an important part of this is that it's not about *conscious* familiarity. "Indeed, the mere exposure effect is actually stronger for stimuli that the individual never consciously sees."

So, how do you create marketing that's subconsciously repetitive? It's much like the magician who calls attention to his right hand while his left hand is busy (and, if you pay attention, obviously) doing something else. It wouldn't be much of a trick if we were paying attention to his left hand. The trick works because our attention is shifted away. So in our marketing, we have our ad or offer, but then we've also subtly built in the clues we really want them to pay attention to. This may be a comparison to a competitor, or new system made to feel like a known, reliable one.

But by shifting it away from the obvious focus, we are actually increasing the power of the mere exposure effect.

Factor 2: Anchors

In many ways, an anchor is a throwaway. It's a bit like the pawn in chess. The pawn plays an important role. It runs interference. But it's expendable. It was never designed to win the game. In marketing, anchors fill a similar function.

Anchors provide a mental frame of reference for our audience. By giving an anchor, we set down a point—a point that could be completely off base, or even arbitrary—but everything that follows will be judged in relation to that initial point.

In sales, a common anchor is to throw out a high price. The customer may balk. And that's okay. But once that number has been put out, it sways all subsequent numbers. If a customer has a figure of $20,000 going in, a salesperson may use an anchor number of $80,000. It's absurdly high compared to the expected $20,000, but now in the negotiation process, the salesperson will be able to come down to a much more "reasonable" price of $40,000. Imagine going from $20,000 to $40,000, that's an impossible uphill battle. But by anchoring higher—even if ridiculously so—the conversation has shifted from moving *up*, to coming *down*.

If you think these are cheap tricks that don't work in the real world, you'd be wrong.

Chris Voss, formerly the FBI's lead international kidnapping negotiator uses this to establish a price range in negotiations. "The tendency to be anchored by extreme numbers," he says, "is a psychological quirk known as the 'anchor and adjustment' effect."

He continues: "Most people glimpsing 8 x 7 x 6 x 5 x 4 x 3 x 2 x 1 estimate that it yields a higher result than the same string in reverse order. That's because we focus on the first numbers and extrapolate."

Kahneman explains that anchoring is actually a work of both our System 1 and System 2—both our intuitive (subconscious) and analytical (conscious) brain work toward the anchor, which makes it a powerful effect.

For System 1 anchoring acts as a priming effect. In a thought experiment where you were asked: Was Gandhi more or less than 144 years old when he died? "You did not believe for a moment that Gandhi lived for 144 years, but your associative machinery surely generated an impression of a very ancient person." Here's the key: "System 1 understands sentences by trying to make them true, and the selective activation of compatible thoughts produces a family of systematic errors that make us gullible and prone to believe too strongly whatever we believe...System 1 tries its best to construct a world in which the anchor is the true number."

System 2—our conscious side—is a bit more practical. Or lazy. It just stops working after a while and settles somewhere in the middle. And it is the adjustment (from the anchor figure toward what the figure *should* be) that saps the energy from the System 2 side of our brain.

In an article in the journal *Psychological Science*, behavioral psychologists Nicholas Epley and Thomas Gilovich, "confirmed that adjustment is an effortful operation. People adjust less (stay closer to the anchor) when their mental resources are depleted." So when we get tired of calculating the possibilities, we make concessions. And because the anchor is the starting point, we begin our calculations from that place.

Factor 3: Less is More

The old saying "less is more" has been overused to the point of becoming a cliché. But when it comes to your marketing, the mechanism behind the scenes is still very powerful.

Christopher Hsee, professor of behavior science and marketing at the University of Chicago, studied how people would price two dinnerware sets. Set A had a full 40 pieces and Set B had only 24 pieces. As expected, participants valued Set A higher.

But when it was revealed that nine of Set A's 16 extra pieces were broken, participants still valued Set A more, but only marginally: $32 versus $30.

This is interesting. If the participants valued Set B (24 unbroken pieces) at $30 (or $1.25 per piece), then why did they only value Set A (40 pieces, 31 of which were unbroken) at $32? If they were being consistent, Set B—which has a full 7 unbroken pieces *more* than Set A—would have been worth $38.75. But that's not what happened.

But it gets even more interesting. Hsee took his two dinnerware sets to two new groups of participants and asked each group to independently value each set. Set A (including its 9 broken pieces) was valued at $23, while the second group put Set B's value at *$32*.

Look at that again: the broken dishes diminished the overall value *more* than additional unbroken dishes! Or, by trimming out the bad, the overall value increased dramatically. As Kahneman notes, "System 1 averages instead of adding."

In his famous (at least, famous among writers) book, *On Writing*, Stephen King calls this "murdering your darlings." His point is the same as Hsee's experiment. By cutting out everything except the A+ material, you are making the overall product stronger. The same holds true in our marketing. By cutting out only but the very best, we make the full effect much stronger than it would have been with any of the lesser parts left in.

persuasion

This section and the next look primarily at Robert Cialdini's groundbreaking work in the field of persuasion.

In 1984, Cialdini, a professor of both psychology and marketing at Arizona State University, released a book that the market largely ignored. It was called *Influence* (which is a bit ironic, considering how poor its initial sales were). But, in time, *Influence* grew to become the one of the cornerstone books in marketing.

In it, he looks at the seven* principles used to persuade another to do something. In conjunction with the first three chapters of this book, if you apply any one of these principles, or rules, to your marketing, you'll begin to see a change in how your audience responds. And if you can build a system that includes several, or even all, you will have stepped into a natural flow of effective marketing. You will be interacting with your audience on a level

---

* In Cialdini's original 1984 work, he only indicated six principles of persuasion. But in his 2016 followup, *Pre-Suasion* (which is the topic of the next section), he highlights a seventh factor. For the purpose of this book (and smooth reading), I have redacted the reference to his original research to include all seven factors.

that they not only enjoy, but will be eager to reciprocate back with you.

Reciprocation

This "rule says that we should try to repay, in kind, what another person has provided us."

A classic example of this is the Hare Krishnas of the 1970s. They would dress in traditional clothing, walk the streets, humming or chanting, and ask for money. Needless to say, their efforts were not very successful. Until, that is, they changed something.

Instead of simply asking, they began their interaction with a gift. They would approach someone on the street and offer them one of their books or magazines or another small gift. Each member's first job was not to ask for a donation, but to make sure the passerby *took the gift*. "Only after the Krishna member has thus brought the force of the reciprocation rule to bear on the situation," notes Cialdini, "is the target asked to provide a contribution to the Society."

Cialdini found that it did not matter how the one accepting the gift felt—even if they could see right through the entire attempt —if they took the gift, they were on the hook. And as a result the Hare Krishna Society experienced their largest economic gains to date. Reciprocation works as a form of mental balance. When someone gives us something, we are compelled to balance the scales and give something back in return.

Commitment and Consistency

The second rule states that people like to be consistent.

Psychologist Thomas Moriarty staged a series of experiments on a New York City beach. In one set of experiments, a researcher (pretending to be a normal beach goer) would find a spot next to a true beach goer (the subject of the experiment), and then lay his blanket down as if all were normal. After a few minutes, the "victim" researcher would get up and walk away. Shortly after, a second researcher would appear and steal whatever the "victim" researcher left behind.

In only four out of 20 cases did the subjects (who thought they were witnessing a real theft) call out and do anything about the theft.

However, in the second set of experiments, the "victim" researcher did something a little different. Before he got up to leave, he leaned over and asked the subject if they would watch his things while he was gone. This time when the "thief" researcher came by and stole the "victim's" belongings, the number of subjects willing to jump in—and even chase down the "thief"—jumped to an astounding 19 out of 20—that's a response rate increase from 20% in the first case to 95% in the second case.

Consistency is a deep part of our psyche. But we don't always act on it. In the case of Moriarty's experiments, the subjects were *made aware* of that consistency (through their own voluntary admission) only moments before they were presented with the opportunity act. And because this consistency was vocal and in front of another (the subject), the temptation to 'not be true to one's self' was too strong in almost every case.

Social Proof

This is a rule we see played out every day on social media: what my tribe does influences what *I* do.

Social Proof is one of the fundamental reasons why **viral** (a concept we'll discuss again in chapter twelve) exists. But it's also a security net. From Cialdini: "In general, when we are unsure of ourselves, when the situation is unclear or ambiguous, when uncertainty reigns, we are most likely to look to and accept the actions of others as correct."

And while social proof is the highway that platforms like Facebook and Twitter run on, it's also one of the reasons why cults exists. In 1979, Jim Jones used social proof to convince almost a thousand of his followers to drink poisonous Kool-Aid. Granted, there were other factors (like the isolation of being away from home in Georgetown, Guyana), but social proof played a large part in the voluntary suicide of hundreds of people.

It's worth noting at this point that none of these factors or rules of persuasion are good or bad in and of themselves. They are amoral—neither right nor wrong. It is, instead, the user who makes the decision to either help or hurt another. The point of Jim Jones is to illustrate the power of these rules.

This is because social proof is a case of herd mentality. We often think of this as a bad or dimwitted concept. But the truth is, when we look at reviews (from people we know absolutely nothing else about) before buying, we are letting social proof drive our decisions. And when we dress-up for church, talk crude around the boys, or generally fall in line with any other societal norms, we are again illustrating social proof.

Liking

We want to agree with those we like.

Maria Konnikova, in her book, *The Confidence Game*, outlines the eight steps of a con. From the put-up in the very beginning—the moment before you even know the con artists—to the "send and touch" at the very end—when the victim is the one doing the majority of the convincing—the one thing the con artists always has going for her is *likability*.

"Liking is where it starts. When we're skeptical, we're on guard. But when we like someone, our defenses are relaxed."

The phenomenon of liking works because of the halo effect. As Cialdini explains, "a halo effect occurs when one positive characteristic of a person dominates the way that person is viewed by others." Statistically we buy more from salespeople who are similar to us, or are physically attractive, or who compliment us. As naïve as this sounds, this is the halo effect in action.

As a warning, Cialdini notes that we can often see this phenomenon in action when we find ourselves liking a person more than we should. For instance, we've only just met them, yet we're getting ready to (or at least open to the idea of) spending money with them.

Authority

Authority is the sway those above us hold over our decisions.

As in the case of social proof above, we tend to bend to authority. We—at least in America—like to think of ourselves as independent and individual. We're rebels with *or* without a cause. But, in reality, we're not. And we know we're not because of the many conventions we abide by.

As marketers one of the ways we will often invoke authority is by proxy, through *another* authority. Think back to commercials from 1950s when a man in a white lab coat would walk onto the screen and begin talking about the virtues of some over-the-counter medicine or whatever. The viewers were told, generically, that he was a "scientist." And while this exact approach is not convincing today, we still use the same principle to great effect.

When a book has the words "*New York Times* Bestseller" across its top, the publisher is telling you: many people like this, so much so that it has landed on the venerable *New York Times* list. When an author writes a book and quotes experts (as I've done all throughout this book), you're being told: don't take my word for it, listen to the experts. While the method changes, the concept stays the same.

Scarcity
"We want more of what we can have less of."

This is an element we'll talk about in more detail in part two. But for now, know that scarcity centers around the idea of loss. As people, we do not like to lose. In fact, all else being equal, we feel worse when we lose, say, $100 than when we gain $100.

Scarcity can show up in different ways: time, supply, or price. When we build scarcity into our marketing, we force our audience's brain to focus. It's as if we're saying: there's no time to put this off until tomorrow—this opportunity will be gone very soon.

Unity
Unity, or the state of *feeling* unified with another, is the final element of persuasion. But unlike the six preceding elements, unity

acts as a kind of summation of the rest. It is broken into three stages, and for each stage, there are two of the six preceding elements that work best within it. In this way, unity acts more like a summary than a separate factor.

In the first stage, "the main goal involves cultivating a positive association." *Reciprocity* and *liking* are most adept at establishing this, as these both work well with first impressions. Reciprocity gives us a reason to engage more with another, while *liking* is the art of increasing the quality of that interaction.

The next stage is about creating a longterm path. Reducing uncertainty is the primary consideration. For this *social proof* and *authority* are the tools of choice. Social Proof tells us that we are making a wise decision, because those we trust are also making the same decision. And *authority* tells us that those in the know—the experts—are also on board. With these two needs met, we can safely proceed.

The final stage shifts from moving someone who is convinced in their mind (or emotions) to act. As the old adage says: talk is cheap. What you *do* is the greatest reflection of what you believe. And so this stage leans on the factors of *consistency* and *scarcity*. *Consistency* prompts us to actually do what we believe should be done, while *scarcity* gives us the necessary push, in the moment.

By building persuasive components into your marketing, you are bridging the gap to those who *want* to buy from you. Life is busy. People have a lot on their mind. As a marketer, your job is to find the ones who will be better off by using your product, and then remove all of the barriers for them to get started. That is what persuasion does.

pre-suasion

Pre-suasion is a concept that very closely follows—or rather, *precedes*—persuasion. As its founder explains: "by guiding preliminary attention strategically, it's possible for a communicator to move recipients into agreement with a message *before* they experience it."

After Cialdini's work became near legendary, he set out to understand a new phenomenon. Namely: why is it that some communicators are able to use the seven techniques of persuasion more effectively than others? Was it an execution issue? Did some just understand the principles better, and so they could pull them off to greater affect?

The primary difference he discovered is that great communicators are not just adept in what to say, but *when* they say it. Pre-suasion looks at two key factors that help lay the groundwork for successful persuasion: attention and association.

In the 1970's social psychologist Shelly Taylor of UCLA was doing a set of experiments and stumbled onto an interesting find. She set up a pair of research assistants to sit across from each other, and each presented a perfectly weighted argument. On paper each side of the argument was perfectly balanced. And so she wanted to test the effects of having people deliver these arguments: does the same neutral component still hold?

As her study results came in, she began to see mixed results from her researchers. So much so that she even participated in the experiment herself. What she ultimately found was that the *position* of the viewer determines the *judgment* of the viewer. For those facing person A (and seeing only the back of person B), person A's argument was most persuasive. And when the position was flipped (observers seeing only person B's face), person B's argument won.

One might conclude that in real life, person A (for instance) might have better persuasion skills than person B, and so even though the arguments were perfectly balanced, person A's delivery is more convincing.

But in this study, it didn't matter who was actually delivering the argument. What mattered was the focal point of the one making the judgment. Because that focal point is what appears most persuasive. Regarding cause and effect, "The outcomes," writes Cialdini, "were always the same: [whoever's] face was more visible was judged to be more causal."

In a stunning set of studies reviewing the trial and jury opinion of a set of cases, social psychologist Daniel Lassiter found that this same bias of focus carries into the courtroom as well. Regardless of any other variable (e.g. sex, race, age of the subject—or even citizen, criminal, or law enforcement status of the *viewer*), the bias was always present: if the camera was on the face of the accused during an interrogation where they admit wrong (be it true or coerced), then their confession is more often believed. But when the scenario is flipped, and the camera was on the face of the accus*er*, the confessions are substantially less convincing.

What we learn from this is that regardless of place or importance—in both controlled lab environments as well as in real-life life-or-death interrogations—the determining bias of whose case is more persuasive depends on where our attention is focused.

For marketers, the implications are less direct. We can rarely set our audience up in a lab—or worse, a trial—to move them to act. Instead, we must look for the naturally occurring opportunities: the points at which we are most likely to find our audience.

The advertising industry has long understood this, illustrated in the maxim, "sex sells." If the the product is in any way related to sex, such as perfume or clothing, then yes, sex does sell. But there's a caveat here. Sex doesn't always sell. While a series of studies show, unsurprisingly, that individuals spend longer time staring at ads of people of the opposite sex, what's more interesting is that "individuals who weren't looking for a new partner didn't spend any more time locked on to the photos of good-looking possibilities than average-looking ones." In other words, sex works as a naturally occurring pre-suasive trigger *only* if the product is relevant and the person is actively looking for a new partner.

To everyone whose business or organization doesn't lend itself to sexy advertising, this should be a relief. In fact, Cialdini has found sex is only one of six other naturally occurring commanders of attention that are useful to pre-suasion.

The second commander of attention of pre-suasion is the threat. This is common in anti-smoking campaigns, showing graphic images of burned lungs or a recently autopsied body as a deterrent. But negativity alone will often push consumers to reject the message all together—a form of cognitive dissonance. This is a form of despair in which the thinking goes something like: "This is bad, but there's nothing I can do, so I might as well keep on and enjoy myself in the process."

The key with dissuading negative activity is to provide positive steps along with it. An anti-smoking ad that does not include steps for how to quit smoking is unlikely to be effective. But by outlining the new steps, they give consumers hope and a new belief. And "they [use] that new belief, rather than denial, to manager their anxieties." Cialdini continues: "this approach, then, is how public health communicators can best deploy truthful yet frightening facts: by waiting to convey those facts until information about accessible assistance systems—programs, workshops, websites, and help lines—can be incorporated into their communications."

The third commander of attention is changing environments. Pavlov's dogs are famous. Most of us have heard the story of how the Russian scientist Ivan Pavlov trained his dogs to salivate when he rang a bell. By regularly ringing the bell before their meal, they began to *associate* the sound of the bell with their coming meal. But what is less known are some of the footnotes of that experiment, like when he tried to reproduce the experiment to his colleagues. He brought his dogs to them, rang his bell, and…they didn't salivate. What happened? As it turns out, the sound of the bell was not the only association for the dogs. Just as important as the sound was the atmosphere. When the dogs changed locations—even as slight as moving into the next room—the association was reset.

This notion is called orienting response, and it works on people, as well. In fact, it "extends to all manner of bodily adjustments, including respiration, blood flow, skin moisture, and heart rate." Meaning, if our communication affects any of these— and if we can do it either consistently (to train), or tap into an already existing state, we'll be able to pre-suasively prime our audience to our message.

The fourth commander of attention is more of a concept. It is when we change our communication to refer to an individual directly, rather than the group they may belong to. For instance, take this example ad: "After all these years, people might accept that antiperspirants just aren't gonna get any better. They might even accept the ugly stains on clothes from hot days and hard work. They won't have to anymore."

By replacing "the externalizing words *people* and *they* in the opener," notes Cialdini, "with personalizing the pronoun *you*," you'll make the shift to a much more pre-suasive primer. What this is doing is telling your audience not to think of this ad as a reflection of their group, but to think of it as only relevant to them, the *individual*. When the ad applies to their group as a whole—be it as broad as a nationality or as narrow as a small family—your individual will look for cues from the rest of the group. But by pre-suasively shifting it to the individual alone, the ad's naturally persuasive message is allowed to do its full work.

The fifth commander of attention is an idea we looked at in the last chapter: Bulma Zeigarnik's discovery of the focusing power of an unfinished job. By leaving a job unfinished, your brain leaves the task earmarked to return to later. This tells us, as marketers, once we have their attention the point where we break away is critical. Regarding how well ads were remembered, Cialdini notes, "the greatest recall occurred for details of ads that the researchers stopped five to six seconds *before* their natural ending." By cutting just before where our audience is expecting the cut, we leave a story loop open—a loop that will stay open until we close it.

Midcentury, the "serial" was a popular kind of TV show. Each week the protagonist would find himself in a new adventure. During the week's episode, he resolved the issue just in time to land himself into a brand new set of troubles. And, predictably, this would happen just as the episode ends, leaving the viewer to wonder what will happen next. "Adventures of Captain Marvel," "The Hardy Boys," and "Flash Gordon" are classic examples of the Zeiganick Effect in action. Each episode ends with a cliffhanger— the hero's fate pending in peril. And each week, loyal viewers flocked back to see what will happen next.

The final commander of attention is about mystery. And if used well, it can be one you use in most of your communication. But the name "mystery" is a bit misleading. A better way to think about "mystery" is as an interesting topic. This is somewhat of an art. But there are steps that you can follow, and the more you practice, the more effective you will become at it.

Going against conventional wisdom (or appearing to) is a good way to start this. Your audience may be skeptical—and that's okay —but they will be curious. Once you have the initial burst of attention, hold on to it by immediately deepening the mystery. Begin explaining how your message or product could be true, but don't give away everything just yet. Take this time to walk through some common objections. Tell a bit about alternate explanations you explored in your research. And then, finally, pull the sheet off and reveal the answer to the mystery.

Ameriquest Mortgage was officially shut down in 2007, and their subprime-mortgage lending practice was routinely criticized for playing a key role in the 2008 global financial crisis. But before all of that, they ran a series highly successful laugh-out-loud commercials where things were not always as they seem.

One commercial opens with a man with flowers and groceries uses a spare key to enter an apartment. He walks into the kitchen and begins to prepare dinner. As the marinara sauce comes to a boil on the stove, he briefly steps away to light two romantic candles on a table set for two. He walks back into the kitchen and uses his gourmet knife to chop a few last minute vegetables, when the apartment owner's fluffy white cat jumps up onto the stove and knocks the entire pot of red marinara sauce onto the floor. Fearing a bigger mess, the man reacts, mid-chop, by reaching down to picks up the cat from the pool of marinara sauce. And at just that unfortunate moment, the woman who owned the apartment, walks in the front door. Her first sight is the man holding his gourmet knife in one hand and her dripping red cat in the other. The ad immediately flashes the words: "Don't judge too quickly. We won't." The point of their ad was that sometimes we find ourselves in situations that look worse than they really are, and we need people who will hear our full story. They used mystery in a humorous way to illustrate this.

If you have a boring product, like a dental drill or a coffee filter, using these six commanders of attention may result in a little bit of a let-down. So instead, pare them with a lesson. Your lesson could be the value of investing in a good product (*buy ours*). Or, if you're in the nonprofit or church world, the lesson may be more about life application (*we'll help you get there*). By using these techniques to capture attention, you're preparing your audience to be receptive to your message.

So far we've looked at pre-suasive elements that all revolve around *focus,* outlining the six pre-suasive components that increase focus. But there's another side to pre-suasion, and that's *association.*

Neurologically, associations are how new thoughts are formed. We learn best by analogy, because once we've mastered one concept, a whole new concept may take only a little bit of tweaking to understand. Riding a bike is a lot like driving a car. You use the pedals to control the speed. And the speed determines how quickly you arrive (and how dangerous the ride may be). And while you're doing that, you need to keep watch so as not to crash. Both a bike and a car operate on the same principles. What changes is how those principles are applied.

The same ideas carry over into our social world, too. Your mom always told you to be careful about who you hung around with, because she was worried you'd spend too much time with bad kids and become one yourself. Conversely, peak performers spend their time with other high achievers, because achievement begets achievement.

The subtlety of associations is found in all areas of our life. In a 2014 study published in *Organizational Development and Human Decision Processes,* two researchers found that on a problem-solving task, merely making available a photograph of Rodin's classic statue *The Thinker* increased scores by *48%*.

And this is where it really gets interesting for marketers. If we can place seemingly benign images (or words) in front of our audience—words that support our end goal, we have a strong chance of moving our audience. In another case, fund-raisers at a call center were secretly divided into two groups. The first group received their talking points written on a piece of paper. The second group received the same talking points, but on their piece of paper was the picture of a runner crossing the finish line of a race. At the end of the three-hour block, both groups were assessed and the group who had a picture of a runner raised 60% *more* in their three-hour block.

By tapping in to associations we can prime our audience to better hear our message.

The important reminder about associations is that subtlety is important. The moment you call it out for what it is—or craft it so obviously that everyone can see it—it begins to lose its power. This was illustrated in an experiment where researchers polled shoppers, asking them which brands they were most likely to buy. Those surveyed indicated brands with the greatest exposure. However, when the researchers measured which of these brands were actually selling best, the results were opposite from what the surveys told. Those surveyed recognized some of the popular brands—the ones who could afford the best shelf placement—but actually didn't buy them as often. "The most subtly placed brands were chosen by 47 percent of the audience, [while] only 27 percent picked the most prominently placed ones." Simply put, this illustrates the power of subtlety in associations. By moving your message out of the obvious (and anticipated) spot, you are subtly signaling that you are *not* trying to manipulate your buyers into choosing your product over your competitor. Instead, it produces the feeling of trust to your audience.

Both attention and association work in tandem with the seven principles of influence from the previous section. These two pre-suasive concepts should be used to lead your audience to the point of being able to use the persuasion techniques. Like getting a good night sleep before a hard day's work, pre-suasion builds the groundwork for persuasion.

manipulation

Persuasion (and pre-suasion) are questions of psychology and sociology. They tap into the wiring in our brains and the functioning of our societies. These are issues that we are already engaging in and so being cognizant of these features gives us an advantage.

But manipulation is something different. This is a question of ethics and morals. (Ethics being the rules of society, and morals being the rules of God.) This means that *intent* and expectation are the deciding factors in manipulation.

It's hard to talk about persuasion without considering manipulation. After all, each of us has either been taken by a shyster, or we've known someone who has. So to read about how to do this to others can be unnerving.

Let me be clear: manipulation is wrong. And you shouldn't do it.

And, the truth is, genuinely successful companies don't have to resort to manipulation.

One of the best ways to illustrate this is by the concept of homeostasis. In science homeostasis is the idea that a system seeks a stable middle, or equilibrium. In homeostasis, there's no edge. No one side is superior to the other. And if one side ever does get the advantage, it is soon corrected.

You may gain a short-term edge to ripping people off. But you can't run a business like this. Despite contracts and laws, businesses are still run primarily on trust. (Which is why one of the core persuasive techniques, authority, works.)

So, how then does one find an edge?

Simply put: you find your edge not in manipulation but in *application.*

Consider Walmart's use of just-in-time inventory from chapter two. Instead of buying in bulk and keeping stock on site (which requires a lot of space), their inventory management system automatically orders only what they need, when they need it. And because they order so much volume overall, they are able to keep costs low.

Walmart was hardly the first to use such a method, but they were one of the first modern corporations to use it at such scale. And as a result, they positioned themselves a good decade ahead of their competition.

Regardless of your thoughts about Walmart and their ethics, their use of just-in-time inventory (their application) didn't require them to take advantage of their suppliers. In fact, it made them *more* dependent on their suppliers.

By finding an edge through application we create a model that is both sustainable and honest.

highlights

Direction is about intentionally moving a conversation or idea forward. Whether it's you trying to get approval from your supervisor for a marketing campaign, or the campaign itself trying to get customers to listen.

In our society, we give pure logic a pass. We believe that once we explain the logic, everyone will understand and all will be right. But that's not how we're wired. Instead, successful marketers bring in the components of **rhetoric** to give their logic an appropriate context.

Because our brains are wired to take shortcuts to save energy (applying **heuristics**), we are wise to present our information in ways consistent with this programming. That includes familiarity (which builds trust), **anchors** (which give a baseline), and less is more (because our brains average instead of add points of value).

Psychologist and marketer Robert Cialdini has outlined seven different factors to create a persuasive message. By implementing these factors, you are creating an easy bridge to those who *want* more from you.

Pre-suasion is the groundwork that comes before successful *per*suasion. By carefully preparing your audience for your coming message, most of your work will have already been done.

When considering persuasion and pre-suasion, manipulation is a topic that often gets dragged in. But manipulation is fundamentally different. Pre-suasion and persuasion are about motivating your audience to act. Manipulation is about *intent*. You can persuade someone to do the right thing (which is good), or you can persuade—*manipulate*—them to do the wrong thing (bad). In all of this, we are personally responsible for how we use the tools we are given.

Part 2:

tactics

The tools we use to execute our strategies

chapter five
scarcity

O f all the tactics in this book, scarcity just may be my favorite. However, unlike most of those I list here, scarcity is probably the most misused.

As for a definition, **scarcity** is the force that causes our mind to become hyper-focused when important resources become unavailable. There are quite a few components in that definition. So let me share an example.

Pretend for a moment you are a diver and you discover your air supply is dangerously low. What happens next? Your full attention becomes automatically refocused on your air supply. At that moment nothing else matters. And this is the way scarcity works. It takes an important issue and it floods your consciousness with it.

Scarcity, however, is just as dependent on the *feeling* of importance as it is on the actual truth of the situation. Let's change our diver story and say that you misread your gauge and *mistakenly* thought your air was low. Even though you had plenty of air, you *believed* your situation to be dire. So in that moment, your mind—even though it was unnecessary—obsessed about getting more air.

The key point here is that scarcity is first *psychological*. Even if the reason for the scarcity turns out to be untrue, our minds react to it all the same.

In marketing, scarcity is a tool that helps you focus your audience's attention on a specific point at a specific time. And because life is full of distractions, scarcity—if used well—can be how you cut through the noise.

But scarcity is not something you can (or should) fake. It's not a button you can push. Instead, it's about discovering what your audience wants most and then communicating the *limitation* of that want. For instance, if an opportunity really is available for only a limited time, then make sure your audience understands that first. Or, if seats are limited, find a way to let those who want them most know about this limitation. Scarcity isn't a trick. It's about letting your audience know: if you want it, get it now.

The key to building scarcity that works is found in understanding the bandwidth tax.

bandwidth tax

In 2013 behavioralist psychologist Eldar Shafir teamed up with economist Sendhil Mullainathan to study the logic and consequence of scarcity. Specifically, their search was to answer the question: "What happens to our minds when we feel we have too little, and how does that shape our choices and our behaviors?"

An important part of their work focused on the bandwidth tax. We all have limited capacities: limited budgets, limited physical abilities, and limited attention spans. But there are certain external forces that squeeze our capacities even further.

Why is it, for instance, that those in poverty tend to make decisions that keep them in poverty? And why do middle- and upper-class citizens tend to save (or make investments) they can later come back to? Is it intelligence? Saving seems pretty straightforward. So are the middle- and upper-class just smarter than the poor?

Part of Shafir and Mullainathan's research focused on these questions. In one study they found that "simply raising monetary concerns for the poor erodes cognitive performance even more than being seriously sleep deprived." In fact, it only took a "small trickle of scarcity, and all of a sudden [the subjects] looked significantly less intelligent."

It wasn't that the poor *were* less intelligent—it's that the force of scarcity made them *act* that way. Shafir and Mullainathan were able to demonstrate in tangible terms the effects of scarcity on our minds. Scarcity has the ability to actually change how much we can process. The more scarcity we experience, the less efficiently we function. This is why it appears that those with more resources tend to make better decisions. Because, not being under the influence of scarcity, *they do*. This is the bandwidth tax in action.

Bandwidth is a measurement of capacity. If your computer is running slow, it may be because you have too many applications open, causing you to strain your computer's memory. Or, if you're stuck in rush hour traffic, too many cars are trying to move through too few lanes. As a results, everything slows to a crawl. As so it for our minds, too. We have a limited amount of space and processing power. And the more we have vying for our attention, the more it will constrict down anything else we think about.

So when bandwidth—cashflow in the case of the poor; or, our audience's attention to our marketing—is extremely limited, Shafir and Mullainathan demonstrate that our rationality actually goes *down*. This is the bandwidth tax in a nutshell—when we experience an *involuntary* limitation of resources.

What that means for us is that when we communicate with our audience, we must remember that they already have a lot crowding their thoughts. And the more they have crowding, the less they'll be able to process what we're offering.

But this same problem also gives us an opportunity.

For some years now, America has been faced with what many have called an obesity epidemic. Too many people get too little exercise and then eat too much food. But in order for people to want to change, they need to see the problem clearly. People gain weight just a little at a time. And once they notice they've gained too much, it's hard to reverse. Our bodies (and minds) do a great job of keeping the status quo. Curbing something as difficult as the obesity epidemic will take a long-term lifestyle change. This is why simply stating the problem, or the facts, rarely motivates people to change.

However, when studies or public programs begin to show the irreversible daily effects of poor diet choices, and if they can present them in a way that provides immediate benefits, then people are much more likely to take action.

(This, incidentally, is why diets like Weight Watchers, which allow you to eat loads of fruit—even though fruit is full of sugar— are successful. With the bandwidth tax comes a reduced ability to exercise willpower. And so a diet that is completely restrictive is much harder to maintain than one that allows some leeway.)

By using scarcity, the problem can be positioned in a way that causes your audience to sit up and take note. If you have a product or service that you know will make your audience's life better, then using scarcity is a way to cut through the noise (their inability to hear you) and get them to pay attention.

rules of scarcity

When scarcity is misused, the cost is usually just wasted time. But when it's used well, you can tap into a powerful tool that grabs your audience's attention. When building scarcity into your marketing, here are a few rules to keep in mind:

1. Countdown Timers are Short
If you have an event registration, a countdown timer can be a good tool for moving visitors to commit.

However, countdown timers only work when the deadline is *soon*. As in, within a few days at the most. The reason behind this is that your viewers should feel that they don't have any more time to put off their decision. If they have enough time to come back next week, then there is no urgency to act now. A countdown timer needs to highlight the urgency of now.

(As a funny aside, I once saw a countdown timer on a political candidate's website that had over *three-hundred* days ticking away on it. I'm not sure what they were hoping to get out of that counter, but it certainly wasn't creating urgency.)

Countdown timers are a form of deadline. Deadlines—as every procrastinator knows—have power, but only if they're close. And the closer they are, the more we feel their effect.

2. Sales are the Lowest

There is much to say about pricing, and chapter nine will get more into that. But when it comes to scarcity, sales prices can be an effective tool.

When I was in college, I worked in retail for a national jewelry chain. And we would regularly run sales. Before the sale went live we'd have to re-tag everything in the store. If it was a 40% off sale, then all list prices would first go up by about 30%. There was still a discount in there (10%), but it wasn't as dramatic as the advertised 40%. We'd get more traffic than usual. And our numbers would go up, a little. But on the whole, these tactics were not very effective.

Even though our customers may not have known what we were doing, many of them instinctively understood they would still pay about what they would have paid before. And our sales figures reflected it.

When rug stores advertise 80% off, all day every day, the same thing is happening. That's nothing special. It's aways like that. The way to bring scarcity into sales is to offer a legitimately good deal. It has to be a significantly lower price than what they can find elsewhere (or at other times), or the value has to be significantly higher. There's no way to maintain this on a regular basis. The key is to make it unusual.*

---

* In chapter nine, I illustration what appears to be the opposite effect. CEO of JC Penney, Ron Johnson, removed all sales and discounts and offered "fair" prices. Their sales tanked. Why? Their customers felt good when they bought things on sale. But this doesn't create scarcity. Scarcity helps to reach those who were not looking to buy or act. If a retail store had a real 80% off sale, their figures would be astronomical. Not only would the regular bargain hunters be there, but plenty others who know this kind of discount cannot last long will also be in line buying.

3. Exclusivity is Unique

Exclusivity is an offering your audience cannot get anywhere else.

The only catch here is that they have to believe you.

If you offer the lowest price, then you need to provide a justification for why *only you* can offer this kind of price. In the world of Amazon and Walmart (and many others, trigger-ready to price-match), what will intuitively tell your audience that *only you* can truly offer this low price?

If you are providing a service, like consulting or software, what will tell your clients that you are not a clone of your competitors? Even in the nonprofit and church world, why should people give their time and energy to your cause? What exclusive element are you providing?

The only right or wrong answers here have to do with the perception of your audience. If they believe you, then you can invoke the scarcity of exclusivity. If they are unconvinced—even if they are wrong—then scarcity will not play to your advantage.

4. Limited Time Offers (or Last Calls) are Rare

Limited time offers or last calls work when the wait is going to be painfully long (or if ever) until it is offered again.

In the early 2000s I went to an Eagles concert. It was their "Farewell Tour, Part 1," a tongue-in-cheek poke at how the music industry attempts to do scarcity. In this case, the Eagles already had a fanbase ready to buy whatever tickets they put on sale. But assuming your brand has not reached celebrity status, putting out a limited time call signals to your audience that of all the offers they're considering, yours will be expiring soon. They can get the others' offers tomorrow, but yours ends today.

As with the rest of scarcity, to work, this needs to be a real limited-time or last-chance opportunity. A closeout sale is not a ploy to get your year-end sales up. It's the we're-going-out-of-business-and-we-want-to-get-anything-we-can-for-this-stuff pricing. Like the boy who cried wolf, if you talk about great things but don't deliver, your audience will quickly catch on. Not only will you *not* invoke scarcity, but you'll build a reputation as no different from your endless competitors.

case study: starbucks' pumpkin spice latte

Regardless of your (probably strong) feelings on the matter, each holiday season in America, Starbucks offers their Pumpkin Spice Latte. And then for the rest of the year, it's not available.

Is there anything special about the flavor pumpkin spice? I don't think so. To me it's *okay*. It's not the new chocolate or anything. But for many, it has become another symbol of the holidays, and it's special.

The interesting part about this is that a company like Starbucks will do market testing before they release a new product. As a result, some products never make it to the menu, while others (such as the Mocha Frappuccino) become permanent fixtures. However, there is a third category. And these are seasonal items, like the Pumpkin Spice Latte. There's no way to know if early testing results were simply not strong enough for Pumpkin Spice Latte to be a year-round drink, or if paring it with fall and winter (and making it unavailable the rest of the year) makes it more desirable than it would have been otherwise.

But what we do know is that the strategy for this single flavor is bringing in as much as *$80 million* per year in revenues for Starbucks, (and not to mention, its spring-summer void has given way to its very own black market for those who just can't wait). Using scarcity, Starbucks created one of its most popular products ever, the Pumpkin Spice Latte.

chapter six
gamification

A while back I was having lunch with a friend. After we ordered our food, our waters arrived and we started talking. Then, abruptly, as if she'd just remembered something, she said, "Excuse me for a sec," and pulled out her phone. "I need to water my plants."

"You water your plants from your phone?" I asked, not bothering to hide my interest.

"No," she laughed. "It's a game. Whenever I drink water, I water these plants in this app, and it's a way of keeping track of how much water I drink every day. The closer I get to my goal, the healthier my plants get."

The above example is **gamification** in a nutshell: moving your customers, users, or audience to engage with your product by building game mechanics into its usage.

The term gamification has only been around for a few years, because it solves a relatively new problem. Once upon a time, text-based newspaper ads worked because people took the time to read them. Today—and the constant refrain of this book is that—there is so much stimuli, and it's all fighting for the attention of your audience. Yet, regardless of the plethora of shiny new things the market produces, gamification is an approach that cuts through the noise.

Gamification is why Facebook is so addictive. It's what the U.S. Army has begun employing in shopping malls. And it's how mint.com has made the daunting task of creating a personal budget so popular.

But what *is* gamification? On the surface it may seem to be simply adding game-like features to your product. Which is simple enough. But Forbes contributor Brian Burke, writing on the topic, estimates that about *eighty* percent of businesses attempting to use game mechanics are not actually meeting their objectives. As Gabe Zichermann and Joselin Linder in their book, *The Gamification Revolution*, write, "gamification is a process, not a product."

This concept is central to building a successful user experience. It's not about winning: it's about the journey of mastering a new skill. That's the core principle that makes gamification successful. The more you can draw your audience into the *process* of your product or service, the more they will invest their time. Gamification is how you do that.

the 5 (business) elements of game

Regardless of how game-like your product is (or isn't) there are five elements you need to consider when building gamification into your brand. They are: points, badges, levels, letterboards, and rewards. By weaving these into the use of your product, you'll find your audience wanting to engage more.

Points

Points are the smallest way of showing progress. And showing progress is what motivates your users to stay connected. As Zichermann and Linder write in *The Gamification Revolution,* points "track behavior, keep score, and provide feedback."

Points in a business environment usually look like some form of currency. I get points on my Amazon Visa card. Some purchases get me more points than others, and all of them can be used as cash on Amazon (or just cashed out). But points also define how your users interact with you. Kevin Werbach and Dan Hunter note in *For the Win* that points can be used to define competition, they can be used for the "dopamine drip of constant feedback," or they can be used to show progression *without* being promoting competition.

Points are good for showing progress. But points are a bit limited by themselves, and so they are often used with badges.

Badges

Badges are a form of identity. When I completed a certification recently, the certifying agency send me a digital badge I could put on my website or in my email signature. Badges are a way of *qualifying* points. It tells everyone else you've earned a significant amount of points.

Badges, write Zichermann and Linder, generate "a touch point for the gamified system to communicate with the users, bringing them back into the experience." Because badges show accomplishment, they use the persuasive force of consistency (from chapter four) to move their holders to re-engage. "After all," goes the thinking, "I've put this much in, I may as well continue." And so badges have the dual ability to show the outside world what a certain amount of points earn, while also working to keep the badge holder engaged.

Levels

Like badges, levels communicate identity, but they do it through community. While an individual gets a badge to stand out from the crowd, being at a certain *level* signifies camaraderie with others at that same level.

Academic degrees ("Phd"), staff titles (like "pastor" or "executive director"), and customer labels (such as "preferred status" or "beta testers") all act as level designators. Levels indicate hierarchy and "provide users with a sense of progress and accomplishment." This comes in handy when you need to mobilize your audience to act on your behalf, such as with influencers or brand ambassadors. By providing a certain level of accomplishment, those lower on the hierarchy look to higher levels as authorities within your brand. Alternatively, those higher up feel the achievement of being an elite member.

Letterboards

Letterboards are a public display of status. But unlike badges and levels, letterboards are reserved for the high scores. By getting to a letterboard status, a person (or group) has signified that they are elite.

But letterboards can backfire. If they are the only element in your gamification, they can be demoralizing, acting as a display announcing everyone who's *not* a winner. "Several studies have shown that introducing a letterboard alone in a business environment will usually reduce performance rather than enhance it," write Werbach and Hunter.

One way to build a good letterboard is to emphasize *several* factors to compete on. Doing this allows people with different strengths to excel. But it also removes the focus of a singular competitive point. If, say, three to five competitive factors are registering, it's easier to show multiple legitimate winners who would not otherwise be listed. Doing this increases morale of your team or audience by communicating that different strengths are valued.

Rewards

Everything to this point has been peer-focused. Rewards, on the other hand, are primarily user-focused. It's the benefit of playing.

"The goal of a good gamified system," writes Zichermann and Linder, "is to offer a set of rewards that activates the users' intrinsic desires, while leveraging external incentives and pressure where appropriate." This is important, because it will ultimately be this intrinsic—or internal—motivations that drive your audience. (This is similar to the internal problem from the "How to Tell Your Brand's Story" section in chapter three.)

However, it will be the external elements that others see, and that in turn motivate others to join in. Zichermann and Linder conclude: "Gamified systems lean heavily on psychological and virtual rewards for driving meaningful behavior." Rewards that are both merit-based and achievable can drive this kind of engagement.

game theory vs gamification

As you learn more about gamification, you may come across a similar term called "game theory." These sound similar, but they are actually very different.

While gamification is the process of pulling game mechanics and design into business, game theory is a theoretical strategy between intelligent parties. It was pioneered most recently by John von Neumann in the mid-twentieth century with an application for military and political purposes.

Gamification looks at behavior and habits, while game theory is based on mathematical models. The two are sometimes confused but have very little overlap. In business and marketing, gamification is most often what you're looking for.

case study: nike+

We think of brands like Nike as being market leaders. And in some markets, they are. But in 2006, Nike's decades long track record was lagging significantly in the running shoe market. Brands like Asics and New Balance had become the go-to shoes for serious runners.

As a brand for serious athletes, Nike decided they needed to either get out of the running shoe market altogether, or re-think how they were engaging their audience. They picked the latter.

In 2006, they began using game mechanics. And in three-years' time, they became the undisputed leader in the running shoe market. How did they do it? They put a small chip in their shoes which synced with an app on your phone (or one of their watches). And from there, you could see your run progress. A social media connection lets you share your best times with your friends to like and comment. And you can also challenge other Nike+ users to a race. Through this system, they used all five elements of gamification.

At its heart, Nike "leveraged a very simple concept—beating your personal best—to create a kind of rapid gamification system."

But Nike did not only capture the serious running market, notes Zichermann and Linder. With only "9 million frequent runners in America...Nike's major market is composed of the 38 million Americans who casually run or jog at least once every two months." By gamifying their product, they were not only able to pull ahead and beat their competition, they were able to expand their market in the process.

chapter seven
content marketing

Content marketing is when you use your product as its own marketing by giving away a valuable version of it for free.

At first, this seems antithetical to healthy business. Business, after all, is about exchanging something of value (your product or service) for something else of value (money).

And content marketing still depends on that. But the *purpose* of content marketing is about gaining something else: trust. Before your audience decides to buy, they decide to trust you. And content marketing is a powerful tool for building trust that with your audience.

Here's what it looks like. If you're selling a service, content marketing may be the exact same service, but free for two or three months. Or, if you're a nonprofit or a church, it could be a blog or even a (free) book that aligns with your audience's values. If you're a business with physical inventory, like a retail store, content marketing can be an ebook or video series that helps your audience solve a problem similar to what your products do.

In each of these cases, you are creating good product that either is, or directly aligns with, your product. Content marketing then gives your audience a way to try it before they buy it. And if it's a good fit, they will trust you and come back for more.

The question most will struggle with is: How *much* should I give away for free—and when should I start charging?

how much should you give away for free?

If you give away too much, there will be no reason for your audience to buy anything (this holds even if your product is nontraditional, like community involvement—you're still asking your audience to *do* something).

But on the other hand, if you don't give away enough, you either won't attract any interest, or worse, your offer will come across as cheap or stingy. Neither of which will build trust.

The traditional advice is to give away the *why* and then sell the *how*. By giving away the why you spend your time emphasizing the importance of your product or service. If for instance you sell vacuum cleaners, then your why may be the health concerns of un-vacuumed floors or the annoyance of their current vacuum. By focusing your content marketing on the why, you build the need.

The how then becomes your product: how do you want to make your house healthier (or easier to maintain)? "Buy our vacuum! It will solve this problem for you."

The traditional advice here is not bad. But with ever-increasing competition in our world, I suggest taking it one step further. And that is: give away a good chunk of the how, too.

The catch is that you always have to be leading your audience to something better.

For example, if your business has physical inventory, how much could you give away? Could you create a starter package? And what would encourage your audience to come back and get more?

The value of giving away more than your competitors is that it generates word of mouth, because as Seth Godin notes, you're creating something remarkable (more on this in chapter eleven).

If on the other hand, you are a church or nonprofit, how much of what you offer can you deliver to your audience before they need to make a commitment?

For content marketing to work, you need to have two things in place: excellent quality and a built-in reason for your audience to come back. If you create quality content, you're building trust in your product or service. And when there's a good reason for them to come back, you've created marketing.

common hurdles

Because there's a subjective line between how much to give away and when to begin charging, content marketing can be challenging. However, if done right, it can also be very rewarding. Here are a few common hurdles to content marketing.

Fizzle without a plan

If you've ever been to a company's website, clicked on the blog tab, and found three lonely posts, all from over a year ago, you've seen a company in the process of failing at content marketing.

The difficult part of content marketing is that it often doesn't *feel* like you're creating anything of value. When you create a widget that costs you five dollars and then sell it for ten dollars, every widget sold feels like progress. But when you write a blog post, share it on Twitter, and then see *no* money come in, it can feel like you're wasting your time.

The way to succeed in content marketing is to have a plan. First, schedule a time on your calendar when you're going to create content. This is a long game, so it needs to be a regular part of your week or month.

Next, determine how it integrates into the rest of your business. Are you writing articles that point to products you sell? Does the video solve a reoccurring problem your audience faces? The more your content integrates with the rest of your business, the stronger your marketing will be.

Internal Disagreements

Because of the perceived risk ("giving it all away") of content marketing, all of your decision-makers need to be on the same page.

If you have a team divided on how to approach content marketing, or if your whole team is not sold on the value of it, it's best to stop and get everyone on the same page. If not, the decision to give away valuable content will be seen as a waste of time, or worse, lost profits, instead of a form of trust-building marketing.

The same thing applies to unilateral decision-makers—for content marketing to work, you need to be completely bought in. If you have doubts, stop, collect some data or talk to others already doing it, and address those issues. If you let those doubts grow, you'll quit before you begin to see fruit.

Content marketing is a long game. So you need to have a plan, and you need everyone to be bought in.

When Quality Isn't Good Enough to Sell
The last major hurtle to content marketing is making an inferior product.

This bears repeating: if the quality of your content is not at the same level of what you're asking your audience to buy, then you're not actually building trust. If anything, you're doing the opposite —you're teaching them to *expect* less quality from you than they would get if they bought.

Content marketing is something I use in both of my businesses. If you visit fiveroundrocks.com (where my company helps entrepreneurs and nonprofits with their marketing) you'll be able to download my free guide to help you reach your audience. When you do, I'll send you a series of in-depth articles so that you can continue to grow your business.

If you visit my other business, joefontenot.info (where I write about practical spiritual growth), you'll see a similar model aimed at a very different audience. While Five Round Rocks is primarily about marketing and building websites, joefontenot.info is a series of meditations on spiritual growth. The business model here is that I write free articles and then sell books.

Both of my businesses use content marketing as a key component of the sales funnel (a topic we'll look at in the next chapter).

case study: scott adams, dilbert, and politics

Scott Adams is the creator of the Dilbert comic strip. He is probably one of the most famous living cartoonists. How does a cartoonist—famous or otherwise—implement content marketing into his business?

If you're unfamiliar with Adams, you may guess things like: giving away exclusive cartoons for subscribers, or sharing behind-the-scenes access to new sketches. But no, Adams uses content marketing in his business through writing about politics.

At first, this seems a bit strange. Your content marketing, after all, should be connected to your product. So how does politics connect with comics? In Adams' case, it comes down to *who* reads his comic strip. Dilbert is an office worker in a large corporation. Many of the punchlines revolve around the silly things bosses do and the odd parts of corporate America.

Now compare that to what Adams blogs about: the silly things politicians do and the odd parts of national governments.

While his comic is satire and his blog is commentary, the parallel is clear: a big chunk of the audience who laughs at his comics simultaneously nod their heads at his blog posts.

So, do Adams' blogs directly lead his audience to read more of his comics? Perhaps. He does occasionally include comics in them.

But more than likely what his comics and blog posts do is support his *brand*. The real product Adams is selling is not a comics or blog posts, but his own personal brand—which he monetizes through books and speaking engagements.

This is the commitment.

This is when your potential customer does what you've asked them to do. They buy your product or service. Or they join your community. Until the buyer gets to this stage, they are not actually a 'customer' or member. Up until now, they've only been a prospect.

5. Re-buying
This is the golden area.

The re-buying stage is when a buyer likes your product so much they decide to buy again. In the context of a church or nonprofit, this is the volunteer who takes a significantly more active role.

The reason this stage is golden is because you no longer need to do any selling. Buyers who make it to this level are already sold on your work and they are proactively seeking more of it.

Your only job at this stage is to equip them to keep using your brand. They'll naturally tell others (**word of mouth**), and this will directly impact others in the evaluation stage. The more members of your audience who move to the re-buying stage, the less *you* have to promote yourself.

Let's look at two quick examples of these five stages in action. And to help illustrate how all five steps show up, regardless of the size commitment, I'll use the extreme examples of buying a Snickers bar and buying your first house.

In the case of buying a Snickers bar, stage one is knowing what it is. Because a Snickers bar is so ubiquitous in America, this happens automatically. In the checkout line, the impulse is to get something sweet. And so in the moment between picking up the Snickers and glancing over the rest of the chocolate bars, you make a snap-judgment evaluation (stage two). The borrowing stage (stage three) is almost just as quick. If you've enjoyed chocolate in the past, your mind prepares to enjoy it again. The craving gets stronger as you decide this is what you want. (Notice next time this happens to you. It's very difficult to put that bar back once you've already picked it up. You may also begin to salivate a little or feel a touch of hunger. This is the power of the borrowing stage.)

Lastly are the purchase and re-purchase stages (stages four and five). If this is the first time you're eating a Snicker's bar, and if you like it, the impulse to buy again is reinforced in the positive experience.

For buying a home, the stages are a bit more obvious. You research (stage one) by deciding between renting and owning. And then, once you've decided to buy, how much can you afford? And what other hidden costs will you have to pay for? Next, (stage two) is about deciding where you want to buy, what kind of house, and what other factors (like nearby schools) will matter. In borrowing (stage three), you begin to visit houses for sale, and you may even talk to the seller about price. But you haven't yet committed. Finally, you buy the house (stage four). And ultimately, you'll sell that house and buy another one later (stage five).

The five step path to purchasing is the process each buyer goes through. Before you can build a sales funnel that works, you need to understand what these stages look like for your audience.

so what *is* a sales funnel?

If content marketing is about producing trust through volume, then a sales funnel is about guiding those same potential customers to the point of buying.

That said, any system that moves potential customers further down the path of purchasing is a sales funnel. Simultaneously, a sales funnel helps you separate those in the crowd who *will* buy, from those in the crowd who won't.

In short, a sales funnel is not a thing, but an idea or system. And how it shapes up is entirely dependent on your business model and what will move potential customers to the point of buying.

But creating a sales funnel doesn't have to be difficult. Here's a real-world example: if a novelist writes a new book, and then wrote a series of posts on her blog about that novel, and then asked some of her friends to share these posts on social media, she's just created a sales funnel.

Here's why this works: of those posts that were shared by her friends, some of *their* friends will click to read her blog. And then, the ones that like it will be inclined to buy her novel. (In the meantime, there will be a bunch of people who ignored those blog posts. And then, not all of those who do click to read will buy. This is very normal, so don't let that side get you down.)

Some at this point want to know: why not just skip the blog posts and ask everyone to buy the book? The answer is the path to purchasing. Our novelist's friends' friends don't know her yet. Her blog posts provide the ability for them to get comfortable with her and her writing (product) before they buy.

The other component of a sales funnel is measurement. Beyond just creating a path to purchase system, a good sales funnel needs to tell you how well it's performing.

Your audience will always be changing, and your product or service will be changing over time, too. So there's really no such thing as a static system. And so without a way to measure how many people are moving through the path to purchase (Is that number increasing or decreasing? And are some points doing better than others?), you won't know if you're doing better or worse. The tools and techniques you use in your sales funnel should tell you this.

For instance, continuing my novelist's example, some posts will resonate more with her audience, and they'll drive more people through the purchasing path. While other posts may be more sharable, but for whatever reason don't drive traffic. In this case, the latter still helps on awareness, but it doesn't do well for creating actual customers.

And then, once they get to your page, do you have a good conversion ratio (visitors to buyers)? If you change the text or images, does it get better or worse? These are the kinds of answers a good sales funnel will provide.

A good tool for measuring this is called a **landing page**. This can be a page on your website or through a service like leadpages.net. And it is entirely customized to your offer. So if you run an ad, you'll point that ad to your landing page, and it will address the promises of the ad. Or, if (my novelist again) wants to share her book in addition to her blog posts on social media, she can create a landing page that is dedicated to her book.

The primary job of a landing page is to remove distractions. If you use your own website, be sure to remove the top menu and footer menu (so that your visitors don't get distracted). You want to give them the best chance possible on following through with why they clicked. A landing page does this for you.

A sales funnel gives you a path for getting new customers and then helps you gauge how you can increase the volume on that path.

how do you build a sales funnel?

A sales funnel begins at the broadest level of interaction—with your *possible* audience—and then narrows until it reaches those willing to buy in. The further down the funnel, there will be fewer people still engaged, but those people have a much higher chance of buying. (See figure 8.1 below.)

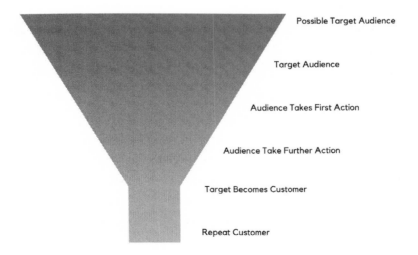

Possible Target Audience

Target Audience

Audience Takes First Action

Audience Take Further Action

Target Becomes Customer

Repeat Customer

(This is similar to the five step path to purchasing, only this is looking at it from your *business'* point of view. You can see the overlap: Stage one is at the top, your possible target audience. Stage two is your target audience. Stage three is when the audience takes their first action—and depending on how much of a commitment you're asking, this may include your audience taking a further step. Stages four and five are when your target becomes a customer and then a repeat customer.)

The way this works is the message you put out at the top is the easiest to create, and it's for the broadest audience. It's the most applicable to the most people.

For instance, if you have a boutique restaurant, you may use content marketing by writing a regular blog. Blog posts about how to find good food or where to get good deals or what to try when you visit foreign countries may be good fodder for the top of your funnel. It is widely applicable, even to those who may never eat at your restaurant.

Once put in front of the widest possible audience, some will choose to visit your website and read your post. It's unreasonable to expect them to search out your restaurant after reading one blog post; however, if the content is good, and if they're the right audience, it's *not* unreasonable to expect them to subscribe to get more articles. Especially if you have a good hook, like an eBook or some other piece of value for everyone who signs up.

After they have subscribed, your blogs will regularly show up in their inbox. Still many will not buy, but that's okay. The funnel narrows as it moves downward. The further down, the fewer people who are interested. But, in that same way, the further down, the higher the probability that those still interested will buy.

Finally, at the bottom of the funnel, your audience buys. And, if you've set up your business model for it, they'll buy again.

Using the above illustration as a guide, below are common ways to build out your sales funnel.

Possible Target Audience

This is where you separate those who *are* your audience from those who aren't.

Social media is a great top-of-funnel device. It's a way to talk to many people at the same time, and those who bite show interest. One of the rules of thumb for social media is that it works better when you don't sell. Social media is a lot like being in public. If you walk around and only talk to people in an attempt to get them to buy—or worse, you don't even talk to them, you just shout "*buy now*" all the time, you won't see many results.

If, on the hand, you use social media as an opportunity to build relationships, and to help, you'll be known as a real person, and you'll be valued for your contributions. In this way, you're using social media to build trust with those who wouldn't otherwise have the chance to interact with you.

But social media is not the only top of the funnel location. Any pool where your audience *may* be found is a candidate. And this can be offline, too. If you get the chance to speak at a conference, this would be a great top of funnel opportunity. If you get another kind of public exposure, like hosting a community event, this would be another top of funnel occasion.

Target Audience

This is the group from the top of the funnel that your product or service can actually be a benefit for. However, while all of your target audience is capable of buying, as I've mentioned, many ultimately will not.

To move your target audience to a point of buying, you need to begin speaking to their pain. On social media, the blog post or video you shared would become an opportunity for your target audience to engage. When you speak at a conference, leaving a little bit of the 'pain' you talk about unsolved allows you to offer a solution back on your website. By letting the listeners know they can go to your site and download your free eBook on that issue, you've created a genuine incentive for them to move forward.

Audience Takes First Action

This is the signup. Generally, this doesn't cost any money. And it often doesn't cost too much time either. It's easy and has a very low barrier to entry.

However, when a person signs up to your email list, they are communicating to you: I want to hear more.

The other benefit to an email list is that you can control it. Unlike on social media where algorithms control who sees what, on your email list, you can control your message, and, if you're sending valuable content, a much higher percentage of your audience will see it.

Audience Takes Further Action

If you have a big-ticket product or service (thousands of dollars), this will be a small cost (say, under a hundred). If you have only smaller-ticket items or services, you likely won't need this step.

For the bigger purchases this step separates those who just want free things from those who actually want what you're selling.

What is important here is that the small purchase be similar to the large purchase. If you're selling custom software, then the small purchase needs to be a similar kind of software that addresses a limited form of the same problem. If your small purchase is unrelated to the larger, then you're not really gaining any indication that the buyers of the smaller products will want the larger.

Target Becomes Customer

This is when your audience buys.

Until they reach this point, they aren't really customers. They're potential customers, but it's not until this point, when cash changes hands, that they've truly bought in. (If you have an expensive product or service, the same is true, because the small product only exists as a way to move them to the point of purchasing the larger.)

Repeat Customer

This is when a current customer buys again.

The reason this is in the sales funnel is because this is the most economical customer to have. You spend very little to get the person who is already a fan of your work to buy again. Ultimately, you want all of your customers to get to this point. The more of your audience you can get here, the more you can focus on other things.

There is one more thing to consider when you are building a sales funnel. And that is the **downward forces**. This isn't so ominous as it sounds. If you glance back at the sales funnel (figure 8.1), you'll see that a person moves from the "possible target audience" stage all the way *down* to the "customer" (and hopefully to the "repeat customer") stage. In each of these there needs to be an *incentive* for them to move farther.

For instance, take again my novelist. Why would a person who's subscribed to her email list choose to buy her book? What *motivates* that next action? This question of motivation is the heart of the downward forces notion. When you build your sales funnel, each step has to be a logical continuation of the last.

An easy way to begin is to think first about the end result. Then think: What is blocking them from getting here? And then, What barrier is before that? Keep asking until you get to the beginning.

My novelist's first problem is that she doesn't have an audience who knows about her. And when they do know about her, they may not like what she writes. And when they do like what she writes, they may be too busy and forget to buy her book. So in each step of her funnel, she needs to make sure she's *solving a problem* for her audience.

If the steps of your sales funnel are not logically connected, then it is unlikely that your sales funnel will be very effective.

case study: mailchimp

MailChimp is an email auto-responder service. That means, when you subscribe to an email list from a brand you like, a company like MailChimp will automatically start sending you emails on behalf of the brand you subscribed to.

One of MailChimp's most effective top-of-funnel awareness techniques comes with their free plan. MailChimp is especially good if you're building your list from zero, because the first 2,000 subscribers to your account are free. The only catch is that your emails go out with a little MailChimp badge at the bottom. So everyone who sees your emails sees that they were sent through MailChimp (which acts as an endorsement from you for MailChimp).

When you visit MailChimp's website, their home page is built as a landing page. They assume you are *not* a current user and that you need to be converted into a customer (see in figure 8.2 how the two most prominent calls to action are "sign up free," while "login" is small and off to the side).

The secret to MailChimp's sales funnel is that their "free plan" is really their opt-in—mid-funnel, before you become a customer. So you can use MailChimp and still *not* be a customer. But when you sign up, they will begin sending you emails on their features (some of which require a paid account), and when you design your emails, you'll see options you can also only get when you pay.

MailChimp takes a lot of the risk out of moving from a free to paid plan. Instead of requiring a big chunk of money, they let you either buy credits a little bit at a time, or they'll let you select a low

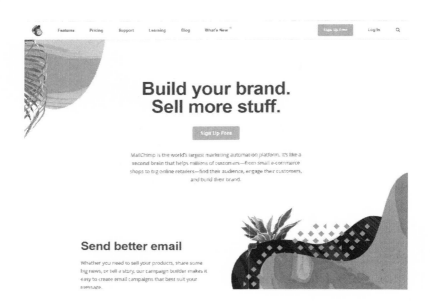

cost plan (if your subscribers are still low). This takes the sting out of buying. And they always let you revert.

When you arrive on MailChimp's home page, each of their tabs at the top answer the same question: Why should I use MailChimp? When you click the features tab, for instance, you'll see how easy it is to automate your emails, and you'll see the other major vendors you can easily connect with (building authority). And then they'll give you an easy way to start running ads that effortlessly put new subscribers into your email list.

MailChimp is not always the best autoresponder on the market. It has limitations. But when I have a client who's building their email list from zero, I will often start them on MailChimp, because the barrier to entry is so low (almost nonexistent), and MailChimp makes the process very simple.

Their sales funnel is built around this same idea: give a good free product up front (**content marketing**), and then build it so that free users do the advertising (**word of mouth**) whenever they use it. Eventually, goes the thinking, free users will like the product enough to pay for the premium features.

When you build your sales funnel, make the move to each new level a no-brainer for your target audience.

chapter nine
price

At its core, price is nothing more or less than a negotiation. Even on static outlets like a webpages where there's no chance for change, price is still a negotiation.

This is because price is a statement of **value**. And when two sides come together in an exchange (your audience buys a product or service, or they donate funds to your cause), both sides are expecting to receive a *greater* value than the one they're giving up.

If I buy a car for $30,000, I expect that what I give up (the equivalent of $500 a month for the next five years) is not as important as what I gain (a new car). And when a donor gives $100 to a charity, they believe that same $100 will be better spent in the hands of the charity than in their own.

So when you put a price on your product or service, you are communicating, above all else, value.

But as we saw in part one, people don't evaluate prices in a strictly rational way. Prices are emotional. And so when we price our work, we must take into account the emotions and environment in which our audience is evaluating our price. This chapter looks at a few key tactics to price in a way that shows your product or service's value.

anchoring

Anchoring is about setting expectation. And, in many ways, an anchor is just a throw-away. It's the entry point to the conversation. But just because it's a throwaway doesn't mean it's without value. In fact, there's quite a good use for it.

In an experiment, Drazen Prelec, professor at MIT's Sloan School of Management, asked a group of his MBAs to set the price for a bottle of Côtes du Rhône wine and then bid on it. The only catch was he first asked them to write down the last two digits of their social security number before they wrote down their bid on the wine. And the results were interesting. Of the fifty-five MBAs who participated, there was a strong positive correlation between the price each MBA bid and the last two digits of their social security number. In other words, the higher their anchor number (the last two digits of their social security number), the higher their bid for the wine was.

This is a consistent pattern we see in pricing: the first number becomes a standard for what follows.

But what's even more interesting is that this holds *regardless* of how extreme the anchor is. Chris Voss, the FBI's former top negotiator for international hostages, says "the tendency to be anchored by extreme numbers is a psychological quirk known as the 'anchor and adjustment' effect." Even if we know the first number is far off base, we still use that as a *basis* to move to what we believe is correct.

Dan Ariely, professor of psychology and behavioral economics at Duke University, adds an important caveat here. When it comes to using a *price as an anchor* for another price, the anchor price needs to be *relevant* to us. Price, he notes, does not become an anchor until "we contemplate buying a product or service at that particular price. That," continues Ariely, "is when the imprint is set."

We can look at relevant prices in one of two ways: prices of similar objects and prices of different objects.

For example, if we see a $3,000 coffee maker, that would not incline us to buy a $120 coffeemaker. The anchor figure is just too far off.

In order for a price anchor to work, we'd need to see our $120 coffeemaker compared to, say, a $300 coffeemaker. Three-hundred dollars is a lot for a coffeemaker, but they do exist. By putting our expensive product next to a more expensive luxury product, our $120 coffeemaker starts to take on some of the properties of the $300 coffeemaker. And at less than half the price, $120 begins to feel like a good deal.

But let's say we've spent the first half of the day shopping for houses in an exclusive gated community. Every driveway has an expensive car. And no one has access to these streets unless they're explicitly given permission. In other words, we've been contemplating luxury all morning.

Now, if we were to see a $120 coffeemaker, we are more inclined to be primed to buy it because the higher prices we've seen all morning act as an anchor for us. Thousands of dollars did not act as an anchor when it was the price of another coffeemaker. But millions of dollars may well act as an anchor if they're *relevant* to us.

the goldilocks zone

If anchoring is about setting expectations, then the goldilocks zone is about setting *boundaries*.

In the child's story of the three bears, Goldilocks never went for the biggest or smallest, or the hottest or coldest. She always went for the middle. And so it is in pricing, too high is too expensive and too low is too cheap. The **goldilocks zone** is about picking the right point, right in the middle.

There's a simple way to do this.

You'll create a **target product**, and then lower and higher **wing products**. Your target product is what you want your audience to buy. And the wing products are the products or services you'll offer alongside your target product.

Your 'wings' need to be comparable. If your target product is a 20 oz bottle of shampoo, your wing products need to be some form of shampoo. Same for services: if your target product is one hour of tech support, then your wing products need to be tech support related. Adding wing products tells your audience: this is too low, and that is too high, but the one in the middle (your target product) is just right.

Here's how you design your target product with lower and higher wing products.

First, determine what your competitors are pricing for a similar product or service. I'm not big on competitor matching (see chapter two). But it is important to know where they are, because your audience will know this.

Next, determine the price and product/service combo you want your audience to choose. This will be your target product. It's important in this step that you take the time to outline the value of this product or service, because you'll use it in the following steps.

From here, create a version of this product that has about half the value, but still cost between 80-90% of your target product. This will be your *lower* wing product. For instance, if your target product is $100 and includes ten widgets, then your lower wing may be $85 and only include five widgets.

You'll create your *higher* wing in a similar way. Increase the value by 10-20%, but increase the price by 50-80%. Again, with your $100 target product, your high wing would be $175, but they'd only get 11 or 12 widgets.

(The reason you'll want to skew higher on the high wing is due to the concept of **loss aversion**. We as people tend to value what we have. The pain of losing $100 is often greater than the reward of gaining $100. This comes down to motivation. For us to move toward gain, the payoff needs to be proportionately bigger than does the consequence of loss.)

What you want your audience to think when they see your three prices is: "If I go with the middle, I can get twice as much as the lower for almost the same price. And it would be *nice* to get more value, but the price for that extra little bit is just not worth it."

The function of the Goldilocks zone is to center your audience's comparison within *your* offerings, rather than having them compare to your competitor. You are, in effect, competing against yourself—but on purpose (and to great effect).

language

The language used in your pricing matters as much, if not more, than the numbers.

Consider the last time you bought something. How did you know you were getting a good deal? I'm guessing you did one of three things. You compared it to something similar. You looked around to see what others were saying about it. Or you looked at what the product had to say for itself.

For Christmas last year, my brother-in-law gave me a bag of Jo Coffee. The little words under the name said: "Apricot, Honey, Crisp Lemon, Clean Finish." I supposed the first three were flavors. But "clean finish?" What does that even mean? I'm still not entirely sure, but I really liked it. And what's more, every time I brewed a cup and drank it, I was thinking about that clean finish. "Will my mouth feel different?" I wondered. And the more I thought about it, the more the experience *did* feel smoother…and cleaner. I still don't know what that means, but when I recommend coffee, Jo Coffee is always on my list.

Dan Ariely and Jeff Kreisler, in their book, *Dollars and Sense*, call this **consumption vocabulary**. The language doesn't change the product, but it does change how we experience it. "From the early days of research on decision-making it has become clear that we choose from among descriptions of various things, not from among the things themselves." This works because "language focuses us on specific attributes of a product or experience."

But consumption vocabulary isn't just fluff. It "gets people to think, focus, and pay attention to, slow down and appreciate an experience in a different way, and then experience the world in a different way."

If you're struggling to get your market to view you as more than another commodity, consider your language. How are you describing your product? And are you using it to tap into what your audience values?

how to price products vs. services

There's an old story about Picasso. Toward the end of his life, he was sitting on a park bench when a woman came up to him. Recognizing the master, she told him what a big fan of his she was. After a few minutes of gushing, she asked if he'd paint her portrait. He kindly agreed. He studied her for a few moments and then pulled out his sketch pad. After some thoughtful consideration, he placed one carefully measured stroke on the page and handed it to her. She was, of course, blown away. His reputation was everything she expected it to be.

And then he said, "That will be 10,000 dollars, señora."

"*Ten-thousand?* You've got to be joking!" she replied. "That only took you a few minutes to create."

"On the contrary, señora, it took me a *lifetime* to learn how to draw that line."

It used to be that physical products could justify a decent margin. After all, they took material and labor and building, and all of that has an obvious cost to it.

The problem we have today is that so much has been outsourced, mass-produced, and given over to the lowest bidder, that it's genuinely hard to justify (on **cost** alone) a reasonable **price** to your audience.

Services—as with the story above—have long known this struggle. "You don't have any overhead," says your customer. "How can you charge that much?"

The lesson we learn from the story of Picasso is that pricing is about value. In the end, a good product or service is worth more than efficiency. Your job as a marketer is to find that value and make sure your audience sees it.

pricing for nonprofits and churches

If you run a nonprofit, or if you are in charge of outreach at your church, you may not feel like you have anything *to* price. But if price is about an exchange of value, then *everything* you do is about price.

The first step here is to determine what your primary ask will be. Time, energy, or monetary donations? Everyone, it seems, wants the latter. But if you get engaged volunteers, will they be more willing to give? And will it be easier to get them to give than an unengaged audience? Think through the workflow. If, for instance, you focus on time or energy, you're not rejecting monetary donations, you're just prioritizing them so that you can get them with the least effort.

Next, once your offer is clear and focused, what can you **anchor** it to? What comparison, to reframe your audience's thinking, makes the most sense? If you're asking for a time commitment, think about how much time your average audience member spends watching TV or browsing Facebook. If you're asking for money, what is something insignificant they could give up to cover your ask? The goal here is not to shame them into acting, it's to put it in perspective for them.

And then, how can you frame your ask (the **Goldilocks zone**)? Can you provide a less satisfying option and then a too-big ask? Is there a way you can show how your ask is the appropriate middle road?

Finally, how can you talk about your ask? What key words or descriptions align with your ask and the values of your audience? Can you walk them through what your ask will accomplish?

Consider these principles when you're building your ask, or *price*, for your audience—even if your business doesn't fit the traditional commercial model.

case study: jc penney

In 2011, JC Penney hired a star executive as their new CEO. Coming from Apple and Target, Ron Johnson was a clear winner. Seventeen months later, Johnson was fired and JC Penney's annual sales had fallen 35% (including a 40,000 layoff).

So what happened?

Johnson started something new. He killed all sales and coupons. For a store like Apple, which is a premium brand, this makes sense. (Retailers sell Apple products not for the profit—their margin is notoriously thin—but for the attraction the product brings in.) But for a store like JC Penney, which caters to bargain hunters, no sales means, well, *no sales*.

Johnson's philosophy was to stop artificially inflating price just so that the stores could knock off "forty percent." On the face of it, he was bringing in a more fair price. What you see is what you get. And in reality, JC Penney's actual prices *didn't* change much during his year and a half. The only thing that changed was their presentation.

But in this process, their audience, who'd come to know JC Penney as a place to get good prices, felt like they were getting ripped off. "What happened to all of the good deals?"

Pricing is not about dollars, it's about value. To think of value in terms of dollars-only, as Johnson did, is a mistake.

chapter ten
website

Getting a website is easy. But getting the right *kind* of website is a different story. This chapter looks at what kind of website you should have. Or, more specifically, what your website should be doing *for* your business.

One of the biggest oversights brands will make is to mistake a good design for a good website.

Take drudgereport.com as an example. The Drudge Report is a hot mess of a website. It's not responsive. Its fonts don't match. And—except for a few oddly placed pictures—it's still *text-based*. If websites were graded on design, The Drudge Report's website would fail. But yet, The Drudge Report is still very popular.* Reddit.com, an aggregator of interesting things on the internet, is another example. They also have an impressively ugly website. But, yet, it's still massively popular. These aren't anomalies. Craig's List, Hacker News, and Wikipedia are other big examples that work in spite of their aesthetics.

---

* Politics aside, I have no idea what drudgereport.com publishes. I do know that its ugly-to-popular ratio is legendary in web design circles.

The point is, while design is important, success is not *dependent* on design. Because today websites are commodities. Your audience expects that you'll have one. And when you do, a good design is expected.* A good design is often not something that causes you to stand out. Instead, it's just the standard.

But if a website is not primarily judged on design, then what is it judged on?

The short answer is that you should think of your website just like an employee.

Each employee has a job that adds value to the company. And when you evaluate an employee's performance, you base it on how well they're doing. But you also know, that the more you put into a good employee, the more you'll get out.

Your website is just the same. It has a job, and your brand's success online will largely depend on how well your website is doing its job.

your website's job

> Brevity is the soul of wit.
>
> - WILLIAM SHAKESPEAR, *Hamlet*

Your website's job is to convert visitors into users.

---

* One may make the argument that ugly websites can actually be a benefit— assuming you're not a designer of some sort, in which case you're website should be well designed. For instance, in the multitude of websites, one way to cut through the noise is by being strongly ugly. Reddit is a good example of this. Their home page maintains the web 1.0 look of text and hyperlinks. However, if you click to their about page (about.reddit.com), you see a modern, well designed site. Why do they maintain the ugly front page?

That's it. That's why they've come to your site. On some level —even though *they* may not yet recognize it—they are trying to decide if you are a good investment for them.

If your site has multiple jobs, you need to make sure these secondary functions are staying well out of the way of its primary job (to convert visitors into users).

The reason your website should only have one job—at least one primary job—is because of focus. As we discussed in part one of this book, your audience is busy and distracted. But when you are laser focused, you separate your brand from the rest of the noise.

Focus then leads to clear communication. When your website is focused on one primary thing, it allows you to say that same thing in different ways. For instance, if you sell counseling services, you can talk about the common objections to counseling, you can share success stories, and then you can offer benefits. Each of these tells the viewer the same thing (come to us for counseling), but in different ways.

Your audience will almost always be interacting with your site before they buy (see the five step path to purchasing from chapter eight). And it's during this decision process that your audience is likely weighing your brand against others. By offering your viewers a clear focus, you're helping them understand exactly what you will be able to do for them, and if they should buy from you.

home base
All roads lead back to your website.

Typically, plugins will only work when you have your own hosting. So if you have a package deal, like wordpress.com (not .org) or SquareSpace, you won't be able to upload your own plugins, you'll just have to use what they have.

These are the foundational mechanics of your website. Knowing this will help you understand someone who can set these things up for you.

One more issue: how much should you be paying for all of this? Most domain names are about $15 per year. Unless you have a ton of traffic, you can get by with $5-30 per month hosting. If you download an open-source CMS like wordpress.org, then it's free. There are also a bunch of free Wordpress themes and plugins for download. But if you buy them, themes are somewhere between $50-250, and most plugins are $20-50.

Taken together you're looking at $75-150 per year, without adding a premium theme and or premium plugins.

If you have an account with a company that manages your hosting and domain and CMS all together for you (like wordpress.com or SquareSpace), then you're looking at anywhere from a couple dollars a month to around $50 per month. (Some specialized companies can go up substantially from here, but you're almost always paying for convenience at that point.)

the 10 laws of building a good website

After building a bunch of websites, studying those who are successful, and seeing for myself what works (and what doesn't), here are the ten laws for building a good website. Whether you're building your site yourself, or you're hiring someone, keep these ten laws in mind.

1. It's not about your brand

This harkens back to chapter three and StoryBrand. You're telling a story, but it's not yours. It's your audiences'.

If your website is all about you, you're like that guy at the party who only ever talks about himself. At best, that's boring. And at worst, you've got everyone looking for an exit strategy. This is not how you want to position your brand.

Instead, your website needs to be about your audience. Where does what you offer intersect with what they need? That is your content. When you stick to this, you will be infinitely relevant.

2. Have a single objective

This is your direct **call to action**. What is it that you want people to do when they get to your site? Do you want them to buy now, call now, or visit? This is the ultimate thing you want them to do.

Many brands get distracted here. They want their visitors to do too much. But if your visitors will only be on your site for a few seconds, a minute or two at most, they're not going to do all of that stuff. If they do anything at all, it's going to be one thing.

One way to find this one thing is to ask yourself: if you could only pick one thing to ask your audience to do, what would it be?

3. Have a path

Once you have your one thing (your direct call to action, or objective), the next step is to create a path for your visitors to follow to *get* to that one thing.

In the woods, a good path has clear markers. These are easy, because it's easy to get lost (or—to step out of my analogy for a moment—it's easy for your viewers to get distracted with the dozen other tabs open in their browser). So you need to make sure your direct call to action is in the right places, and then you need to repeat it frequently.

When you talk about your services, let them know how you get those services. When you talk about other clients you've worked for, let them know how to become one of those clients. And when you're overcoming objections, let them know how you can do this for them too. Each time, you are giving them reasons to buy. Doesn't it make sense to keep those markers of how to buy clearly in sight?

4. Don't forget the soft commitment

Not everyone is ready to *buy now*. In fact, most of your visitors (those who showed up to your site on purpose) probably fall into a middle category: they may like your work, but perhaps they aren't quite ready to buy. So what now?

This is where your soft commitment, or in-direct call to action, comes in. By accepting your soft commitment, your audience is telling you: *I'm not ready today, but I may be tomorrow—keep talking to me.*

So what is a soft commitment? In most cases it's some form of email list. It's a way to continue talking to them, without requiring them to make a buy-now decision yet. If you nurture your email list, over time your **target audience** will be ready to buy.

5. *Spell out how to get started*
In your direct call to action you are telling them *what* to do. But here you tell them *how* to do it.

If you have a lot of steps for someone to get involved, then you want to use this part to simplify that. Give them the big points: *Start here, then do this, and then finally you'll do that.* Give them a straightforward one, two, three to get started with you.

By spelling out the basic steps to do business with you, you are cutting through the noise your audience is hearing. They don't have to stop and think, because you've just done all that for them. Let them know how to start. Don't make them figure it out.

6. *Tell them what they get when they start*
In addition to telling them how to start, tell them *why* they should start.

What's in it for them? How will their life be better? Chances are, you've worked that out a long time ago. That's why you're doing what you're doing. But just hanging up a shingle and a get-it-here sign is not the same as communicating value.

What makes what you do so special? What convenience do you provide? Or, what need do you solve? And how is what they'll give up to get your product or service a good deal for them? Answer these questions on your website, because most of your competitors aren't.

7. Tell them how others have benefited from getting started
In a word, this is about testimonials.

Testimonials signify that your audience's peers have tried you (and, in fact, like you!). It's social proof.

When you add testimonials, you don't need a lot. Just a few good (and short) testimonials works well. As we looked at in chapter four, our brains like categories—you can tap into this by showing your audience what a few of their peers have said.

One caveat to testimonials though, like the first point of this section, is that they *can't* be about you. That's not persuasive. They need to be about the person giving the testimonials.

I've created a guide that will walk you through how to get the right kind of testimonials from those who have worked with you in the past. (You can download it at fiveroundrocks.com/resources.)

8. A way to experience your product now
This can be the trickiest of them all. How can you let your visitors experience your product before they buy it?

It's the trickiest because it really depends on exactly who your audience is and what your product or service is about. For instance, if you're in retail and you sell physical things, it may be an in-depth video or a lush return policy. If you're a nonprofit or a church, where time or action are your direct call to action, it could be a blog or eBook that discusses values you and your audience have in common.

Whatever it is, don't skip this. Do yourself (and your brand) a favor and camp out on this one. Think hard about what you can do to let your visitors experience your world today, even before they leave your website.

9. Use an editor

I don't mean a spell-checker (though, yes, get one of those, too). I mean someone who can objectively look at your site and say: cut all this stuff over here. You need someone you trust who is not emotionally attached to your business to help you stay on track.

10. Add a little bit of failure

This is about what will happen if your audience decides to pass on your offering.

Without failure, there are no stakes. And if there are no stakes, then why should they buy? It's like telling your audience: "Don't worry, what I'm offering isn't that important. If you don't buy it, your life won't be any different." Clearly this is not the message you're going for.

But on the other hand, a website full of failure is depressing. There's a line. Don't overdo it. But don't skip it either.

getting started

As you build your website, keep these laws in mind. My company has websites you can download that incorporate each of these ten laws. You can get those at fiveroundrocks.com/websites. (We include a marketing guide with all our sites so that you get the maximum impact in setting up your site.)

chapter eleven
word of mouth

Word of mouth marketing is a form of advertising. In short, it's when your audience endorses your stuff to their friends.

The paradox to **word of mouth marketing** is that, while it is, hands down, the most powerful form of advertising, it is simultaneously the only kind you cannot buy.

It is completely voluntary.

But just because it's voluntary does not mean that you cannot foster it. Or, in some cases, even create it. The trade off is, what you save in ad dollars, you spend in time and energy.

But word of mouth is powerful, and the more of it you can incorporate, the more effective your marketing will be. This chapter looks at how do it right.

the secret to word of mouth marketing

> The future belongs to marketers who establish a foundation and process
> where interested people can market to *each other*. Ignite customer
> networks and then get out of the way.
>
> - SETH GODIN, Author of *Purple Cow, The Dip,* and *Unleashing the Ideavirus*

Here's the secret to word of mouth: Your audience needs to *believe* your product is really what their friends *need.*

That's it.

The rest of your job is to create a relationship with your *current* audience—and then building a product (or service) that they are genuinely excited about.

There aren't shortcuts here. But if you keep these two markers in site (building your relationship with current audience and then giving them what they love), your audience will naturally pass on the word for you.

how to create word of mouth, part 1

Many of us are creating good work. A lot of us understand what our customers want. And a fair number of us have even carved out a niche in our industry.

But none of these things, by themselves, equal word of mouth. They *are* necessary—but they are not sufficient.

Once you understand your audience, what they want, and then how to give it to them, there are four catalysts you can use to build word of mouth into your marketing. They are: be remarkable, give your audience something to share, enable influencers, and add fans one by one. Word of mouth takes time and effort, but your work will pay off.

Use the these four tools as a checklist for what you are currently doing. If your brand is lacking in any of these areas, shift your focus and make it a priority to improve there.

Catalyst 1: Be Remarkable
Being remarkable is the premise of Seth Godin's "purple cow" concept. We've all seen black, white, and brown cows. But a *purple cow*—that is something we'd talk about.

Until you have *something* your audience wants to share, there's no inherent reason for them to do it. Becoming remarkable isn't impossible. It just takes some thinking.

In case after case, Godin offers, "what all of these [remarkable] companies have in common is that they...are outliers. They're on the fringes. They're super-fast or super-slow. Very exclusive or very cheap. Very big or very small."

In other words, it's not about following the leader, it's about zigging when the market zags, so that people will stop and ask: "What's *that* about?"

But being remarkable isn't about taking exorbitant risks. It's about making a splash. If you're running in sync with the market and looking to your competitors (or your own history) as a template for how you should act, then you're doing the *opposite* of making a splash. You're creating harmony, or flowing *with* the waves.

When it comes to personal relationships, harmony is a good thing. But when it comes to your marketing, harmony is what causes you to blend into the background of the market place.

So, how can bring a purple cow into your industry? What can you do that will cause your audience to pause or double-take?

Nintendo is an examples of a company who built their brand around creating purple cows. One of their first purple cows was the Gameboy. When all game systems were attached to a stationary TV, they created a system you could put in your pocket and carry with you. Next, amid the saturation of new games, they introduced the Wii, a game system that requires you to physically get up and move to play it. And, most recently, they integrated social media and 'live action' with their Pokémon GO. In each case, Nintendo made a fundamentally different shift.*

Catalyst 2: Give them Something they can Share
This is about how you packaging your value for your fans.

Word of mouth requires fans to talk to *non*-fans. Your current fans have the ability to talk about your brand in a meaningful way, because they've experienced the nuance of it. They've used it a lot, and they like it. And so they're natural evangelists for what you're doing.

But when it comes to enabling your fans to share your brand, the message can get confusing. What parts should you fans share

---

* Some argue that Nintendo 64 belongs on this list. However, while Nintendo was the first to beef up their hardware (64 bit) and bring in 3D graphics, this is really a scaling up from where everyone else was. If everyone continues on their trajectory, they'd naturally get there. A purple cow, much like a blue ocean shift, is about making a fundamentally different move.

that will be attractive to a broad enough audience to catch on? If your fans focus on the wrong details, your brand may come across to non-fans as obscure or irrelevant. This is the **curse of knowledge** from chapter one—only this time it's happening with your fans.

In *Free Prize Inside!* Seth Godin again gives us the answer. By building a 'free prize,' a bonus that makes using our product or service more enjoyable than what the rest of the market gives, we create

Here is Godin at length:

> A free prize is the essence of a Purple Cow. Generally, a free prize has two key characteristics. **First**, it's the thing about your service, your product or your organization that's worth remarking on, something worth seeking out and buying…**Second**, a free prize is not about what a person needs. Instead, it satisfies our wants. It is fashionable or fun or surprising or delightful or sad. It rarely delivers *more* of what we were buying in the first place. It delivers something extra.

We find a free prize when we push our thinking to the edge of what's normally done. And "only when you find the free prize," says Godin, "will your customers start talking about you."

Fitbit sold a product that was almost universally needed. Practically everyone in the American market could use more physical activity, and Fitbit was designed to help with that. But how do they communicate their value? Some of their fans were using it because they sat behind a desk all day and needed to get up and get their blood pumping on a regular basis. Others were overweight and needed a regular reminder of how they were doing.

And others still enjoyed being healthy but where busy and distracted, and so often forgot to make time for physical activities.

So Fitbit focused on a singular feature: automation. You don't need to remember anything. Wear this little bracelet, it'll monitor everything for you and let you know when you need to do something different. This way, regardless of your motive, Fitbit was a good match. And when fans talk about it, they talked about the *ease* of use. Fitbit's free prize was the ease and automation for staying in shape.

how to create word of mouth, part 2

Your job as a marketer is to put out an idea worth talking about. That's marketing. When a real person repeats it,
that's word of mouth.
- ANDY SERNOVITZ, Author of *Word of Mouth Marketing*

The first part of word of mouth is having something worth repeating. This is internally focused. The second part is giving it to the right people. This is the part about reaching out.

If you google "how to do word of mouth marketing" you'll see a bunch of articles giving you answers. Most of them include common-sense tips, like "be friendly," or business-based strategies, like "find your uniqueness." These things are fine. But when it comes to taking an active role in building word of mouth for your brand, you really just need to do two things: enable influencers and build fans.

Catalyst 3: Enable Influencers

There are two kinds of people who like your work: fans and influencers.

Fans are those who will tell their friends, but do not have a platform to spread the word exponentially. In other words, they spread your message one person at a time. **Influencers**, on the other hand, do have a platform. When they spread your message, they communicate on a one-to-many level.

For word of mouth, it's important to build relationships with influencers. You do this one-on-one. Influencers get a lot of requests. The more you can customize your offer to their specific needs, the more likely they'll want to share your message to their audience.

Enabling influencers is about finding what their audience comes to them for, and then giving them a way to provide more of it. Think about your own platform for a moment. If someone were to come to you and ask you to share their shiny new widget with your hard-won audience, would you do it? I imagine you would consider it only if it was something that would actually help your audience.

And if you get dozens (or hundreds) of these offers per day, how long would you investigate each to determine if they were a good fit? Given the amount of spam we all get, probably just a few seconds each.

So before you approach an influencer, do the hard work to find out *why* this would make their audience like them more. Lead with that.

Once you've found an influencer that aligns with your brand, begin a real person-to-person relationship with them. Treat it like you're starting a *real* friendship. You're not going to be sending them things to share because it benefits you, you're going to be doing this because it's good for *them* and their audience.

Building relationships like this take time, but it's one of the key elements of word of mouth. When they give their endorsement to the people that already trust them, your brand will be in front of people who have never considered you before.

Catalyst 4: Add Fans, One by One
For as attractive as the idea of word of mouth is, most people are turned off by the doing of it. That's largely because, well, *it's a lot of work.*

Generally when you talk to your fans, you do it on a one-to-many level. *You* are the influencer. And the reason for this is practicality. If you've got hundreds (or thousands) of people interacting with you and your work, it's just not possible to give them all a thoughtful and detailed response. And so it makes sense to talk to them in a mass way (for example, responding to common questions with a single blog post). And, generally, people understand this.

But when it come to generating word of mouth, this principle works the other way around.

Because of the expectation that influencers generally don't talk to their fans individually, when you do—and when you add something substantive and relevant—people take note.

Seth Godin, who I quoted twice in the last section, is, by far, one of the largest names in marketing and business today. I emailed him one time, and in within the hour, he emailed me back. It was short and to the point. But I was stunned he actually (personally) replied. Another time, I sent a copy of my first book (which looks at habits for spiritual disciplines) to Richard Foster, an author who pioneered much of the modern thought on spiritual disciplines. A couple weeks later, I received a personal, handwritten letter in the mail. I couldn't believe he took the time to handwrite and mail me his thanks.

In both cases, I was already a fan. The only difference is now I go out of my way to tell my friends about these two. That's word of mouth marketing.

Because this level of interaction can take time (*all of it*, if you're not careful), it's important to set yourself limits. Set aside a chunk of time each day or week, and focus on sending personalized direct responses. If you can make it public, that's not bad. But it doesn't have to be. What you're trying to do is show as many fans that they are personally important to you.

What do you do if you don't have tons of fans asking you questions? You go to where your fans are: social media or message boards or even physical places, and you interact. In a non-condescending way, interact and offer your expertise when you see someone looking. In this way, you'll build fans that become the kind that want to share your message.

case study: the $15,000,000 comedian no one knows

Last year, Sabastian Maniscalco made over fifteen million dollars as a standup comedian. The catch? No one knows who he is.

Or, more specifically, the mainstream media doesn't know who he is. Yet—I did some quick googling here—last year Maniscalco made enough to cut the small country of San Marino's national debt by a third.

And he did it by telling people jokes. When tickets for his four shows at Radio City Music Hall went on sale, they sold out in *under thirty minutes.*

The reason we don't know about him is because of his bottom-up approach to marketing. Other comedians, like Louis C.K. or Amy Schumer, often use a top-down approach. They'll land massive cable contracts or movie deals. And while this can work, the chances of it happening are more in line with winning the lottery. And so Maniscalco took a different route.

A large part of his success is due to his fundamental use of word of mouth. When Maniscalco would start out, he'd stay behind and meet everyone who came to see him. It didn't matter if there were twenty people in the audience or two hundred. "To me, it feels like they're entering my home," he said. And so at the end of each show he'd stick around and shake everyone's hand and talk to them if he could. And because this kind of attention is such a rare thing, next time he performed at that venue, they'd all be back, and they'll have brought friends.

Word of mouth is easily the most powerful form of advertising. The problem is that it takes time. And energy. Sabastian Maniscalco worked as a standup for a decade and a half before he started to get traction. And this is illustrative of word of mouth. You need to be in it for the long haul. It can work. But you have to commit to it.

new audiences

I'm not sure the days of build-it-and-they-will-come ever existed. Even if you're a natural salesperson and you've got loads of extra time on your hands, finding new audiences can be one of the more difficult tasks in your business.

Not only is selling your business a skill in itself, but it also takes time and energy, and—most importantly—it takes you away from your actual business, the thing people are coming to you for in the first place.

In the recommended reading section, I've included solid books to get you started on the sales front. But, in the meantime, how does finding new audiences fit into your marketing?

Marketing is the structure or framework that introduces your audience to your brand. In many ways, marketing is the support system for you or your salespeople. And so you want to make sure what you are doing both flows into your system (how your business works), and at the same time can scale or grow.

If your process does not flow into what you've already built (your sales funnel, content marketing, and website), and if it's inconsistent with your approach (using scarcity, gamification, or word of mouth), then it's going to create friction. Your audience is going to be confused and you'll be doing the opposite of focusing and building value.

Likewise, if your efforts to bring in new people take as much or more effort than they produce, you cannot grow. For example, if a new customer costs on average $55 to acquire, yet will only spend $55—or less—then you don't have a system you can grow. It's like living a one hundred thousand dollar lifestyle on only a fifty thousand dollar income. Something here needs to change.

When it comes to finding new audiences, your marketing merges your efforts into the larger picture and then builds a system that can scale.

paid ads

Paid ads are one of the first methods many will use in their marketing. And paid ads can work well. But they're only as effective as the *back-end* they are connected to.

In other words, paid ads work best when they're a part of a system, not a standalone effort. To this end, there are three fundamentals of using paid ads: build a landing page first; treat your ad budget as an expense, not an investment; and be sure to measure everything you do.

Step 1: Begin with a landing page
The best place to start with paid ads is by first building a landing page. From chapter eight, a **landing page** is a page created

especially for an ad or promotion that is extremely focused. It can be on your website or on a third-party service, like leadpages.net.

By creating your landing page *before* you create your ad, you set up a hook (your ad) to then lead into a more detailed environment (your landing page). If your audience likes what they see in your ad, they'll click to get more. Your landing page is where you'll continue to move your audience through the purchasing path.

Step 2: Think: expense, not investment

The catch with paid advertising is that they're hit or miss. It's not a bad idea to buy ads. I currently use Amazon Marketing Services on my books and Google AdWords for several Five Round Rocks products. And both work reasonably well. But they each take some calibration.

The best way to think about ads is as an expense and not an investment. The reason is that paid ads don't always work. And other times, they work, but take some massaging. For instance, if you spend too little, or run a campaign for too short a time period, you may not see good results. In many ways, paid ads are a long game. So pick something within your budget, and be willing to experiment and tweak until you get to an optimal level.

Step 3: Always measure your ads

The last point about paid ads is that you need to be able to *measure* them. Most platforms that sell you ads will give you data: views, clicks, click-through-rate, and cost-per-click. But the most important measurement is the one *you* set, which tells you whether or not your ads are actually moving your business forward.

For example, if your first goal is to build an email list, then you'll want to know how much each new email signup costs. You'll also want to know the ratio of those who click to those who subscribe.

Once you have a baseline, ask yourself: Can you change the landing page text to make this more favorable? What about the ad —does it align with your landing page, or the product you're delivering?

Alternately, if your goal for ads is to sell a particular product, begin by comparing its baseline sales to the sales since your ad has been live. How much does it normally cost your business to sell a product? Is what you're spending on ads for these additional sales bringing that total cost down? Or driving it up?

There are a lot of things you can measure, but the only things you *should* measure are what actually move your business forward. Keeping this in mind will help you get the most out of paid ads.

brand ambassadors

A brand ambassador is someone who already has a platform and *officially* tells potential audiences about you.

In other words—however you pay them (be it monetary or otherwise), its your brand ambassador's job to use their influence to *broaden* your audience.

The way to make this work is to align interests. From the mid-1990s to mid-2000s, Pierce Brosnan was a brand ambassador for Omega watches. During that time he was also under contract playing James Bond, and Omega was the watch James Bond wore in the movies.

But brand ambassadors do not need to be famous. They only need to have an audience that is interested in your work.

In order to find a brand ambassador that will help your brand, think about who already has an established platform with a group of people who would benefit from your product. Then work up an arrangement that favors both you and your new ambassador. From here, it's just a matter of the two of you working together to help your ambassador's audience find you.

audience sharing

Unlike a brand ambassador, audience sharing is a mutual exchange.

If two bloggers have a similar (or symbiotic) audience, they can feature each other to their respective platforms. Typically the value swap is about influence. "I'll tell my audience about you, if you tell your audience about me." And unlike a brand ambassador, this rarely involves one influencer paying the other.

The value here is reaching a new audience faster than you would on your own. (See figure 12.1 below.)

Before you do this, you need to have a couple things in place. You need to have a good sized audience. Without this, it's unlikely another influencers will want to share their audience, because it's not a fair trade. But having an established audience also means that you've got a solid product or service. People have voted with their wallets or their time, and you can use that to leverage your value.

The second thing you need is a sales funnel. It won't do you much good if a bunch of new people come your way and then slip away because there's no easy-entry into your world. Right now they trust you on a vicarious level. *They* don't trust you yet, but they've

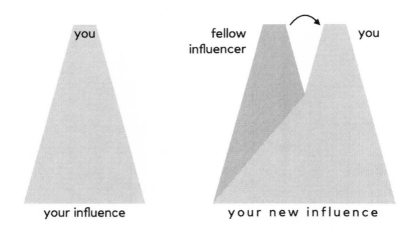

heard, on good authority, that you've got something good for them. Your sales funnel is your hook that introduces them to you. It's the way they can easily (and without risk) investigate you and your brand.

Audience sharing is a powerful way to build your audience fast. But it takes some ground work. A good milestone for growth is to work to the point of being able to have an audience valuable enough for another influencer to be willing to swap with you.

viral

Viral growth is a form of exponential word of mouth where every new customer brings in *more* than one additional customer.

Word of mouth, as illustrated in the last chapter, is a form of marketing that can work. It's something you can plan for, measure, and then adjust when needed.

Viral, on the other hand, is much less predictable. In fact, viral as a *principle* is a good goal, but viral as a *destination* is almost always a waste of time. In other words, it is good to build viral mechanisms into your product and its use, but expecting a viral outcome is not realistic. This is because the factors that result in a viral product or service are largely out of your control.

Consider, for instance, Korean rapper Psy's inexplicably viral 2012 hit, "Gangnam Style." The song and dance are goofy, for sure. The question is not, how did this become popular? (Strange or silly things have become popular before.) The question is, why could he not repeat it?

This kind of anomaly is not new to the entertainment business. For decades Hollywood has had a big business mindset when it comes to making movies. Yet—and not too uncommon—movies will flop. Sphere, based off of Michael Crichton's bestseller (and staring Dustin Hoffman, and Samuel L. Jackson, and Sharon Stone) lost $62 million at the box office. Harrison Ford's K-19: The Widowmaker lost $67 million. And, perhaps the most impressive (though if you saw the trailer it wouldn't have been too big a shock) was John Travolta's Battlefield Earth, which, at $73 million in the hole, lost over *twice* as much as it brought in.

These are massive amounts of money. With individual budgets bigger than the GDP of small countries, it would seem that Hollywood could do a better job of keeping this under control. But they can't. Because what people like turns out to be a hard thing to predict.

In order to create a viral hit, you need to anticipate how your audience will react and then build something that will cause them to fall in love with you so much that they cannot help but tell everyone. And *that* is a tall order.

But this doesn't mean that shooting for viral is wrong. In fact, building viral potential into your business is actually a good idea if you do it right. While you may not be able to guarantee a virality, you can still increase your reach by using viral principles.

The Viral Coefficient
Despite virality's lack of predictability there is still a way to use its *principles* in your business.

In their book, *Traction*, Gabriel Weinberg and Justin Mares define the **viral coefficient** as a way of measuring how likely your product is to go viral. And because the viral coefficient is an equation, you can use it to know when (and where) your business will go viral (or what you can adjust to influence it).

$$K = i * conversion\ percentage$$

K is the viral coefficient. So i is the number of invitations each customer sends on your behalf, while the last part, the conversion percentage, is how many people each i will convert to a user of your product or service.

So for example, say each customer tells five people. And of those five, two ultimately become a new customer, then your viral coefficient formula will look like:

$$K = 5 * (2/5) = 2$$

In this case your viral coefficient is 2. Any viral coefficient above 1 is considered viral—to have an exponential growth curve.

Knowing this formula helps you influence your own viral coefficient. For instance, by influencing more of your current customers to share your message (say, through an incentive), you will increase the *i* part of the equation, which will raise your viral coefficient. Or you could better enable those already sharing, by giving them more attractive tools or tips to pass on, this could increase your conversion percentage and ultimately increase your viral coefficient.

If the math bothers you, think of it this way: the more you incentivize your current customers to share, and the more you give them the tools to convince those they'll influence, the more likely your product or service will reach viral status.

Viral or Perseverance?
Another side to this isn't viral at all. In fact, what many consider viral is actually perseverance.

For a brand or story to reach most of us, it needs to get to a national level. Many brands or stories, however, seem to come out of nowhere. Rapper Jay-Z is an example of this. In the 1990s, he couldn't find a label to sign him. So after much searching, he created his own label. But then he struggled to find a distributer. When he finally brought his first album to market, it was the first most of us had heard of him. However, it wasn't long before Jay-Z's debut, *Reasonable Doubt*, had gone platinum (reaching a much larger audience). Today he's sold over fifty million albums and won over twenty Grammys.

Take a look at figure 12.2 below. As the curve illustrates, for many, overnight success is usually just our perception.

The horizontal line is time, and the vertical line is public awareness. On the far left side of the curve, popularity comes very slowly. Many people quit during this time, because they don't feel

like they're getting anywhere. However, as popularity slowly begins to build, so does momentum. Ultimately, what's popular becomes even more popular (because of social proof), and in some cases, a brand will move into the head of curve (the far right side of figure 12.2 above).

Statistically, most of us will not make it to the head. But if we understand our market correctly, and if we offer enough products to compete in the long tale, the same principles will apply. Through perseverance and calibration, a brand can experience success over time. And many will label it viral when it was really just hard work over a long period of time.

a note on social media

There's a prevailing view that says: because social media is popular you should be using it to promote your business.

But social media is not just popular, it's *ubiquitous*. Facebook alone—albeit, the largest social media platform—has over *1.4 billion* active daily users. That is, one out of every fifth person on the planet logs in to Facebook each day.

I didn't include a chapter on social media here for a few reasons. First, we all know how to use it. So if you're looking for a tutorial on how to do an ad on a specific platform, that often changes by the week. You can find great tutorials for this online.

But the other reason is that social media is less of a destination and more of a pathway. It's true, many people spend a lot of time in these platforms. But it's to interact with friends, share content, or discover new places on the web. In other word, they go there to get what they want. Not just to be there. It's better to think of social media—as its name implies—a *medium* for getting somewhere else. It's a medium for connecting with friends, or sharing and finding new information.

The best practice for social media is to treat it like real life. Would you shamelessly plug your product in a conversation with your friends? Then it probably won't work on social media. What about when you talk to fans who really like what you're doing? Do you spend all your time focusing on *yourself*, or do you try to get to know them more?

Social media is a good relationship builder. This works both on a one-on-one level or a one-to-many level. Use it as the top of your **sales funnel** to provide your audience value so that they'll want more from you.

case study: spotify starts at zero

Spotify is a music streaming service. By the end of 2017, they had 157 million monthly active users. That's roughly the equivalent of one *half* of all the people in the United States (and, at the time of this writing, nearly half of these users are paid subscribers).

But Spotify didn't start out big.

In 2005, Daniel Ek and Martin Lorentzon began working on a new music service that was legal—unlike Napster, which simultaneously introduced digital music to the world and made us "all become thieves," as Jordan Cook of techcrunch.com puts it. But they also wanted to make it accessible. In 2005, iTunes charged a dollar or more per song. While iTunes was revolutionary in some ways, it did not do much to change the economics of getting new music for the end user.

In 2008, Ek and Lorentzon launched Spotify to five countries in Europe. The paid subscription ($10/month) was available, but the free accounts were by invitation only. It wasn't until 2011 that they opened the service up to the United States market. But even then, the free accounts—still exclusively by invite—only gave limited-time access.

Eventually, Spotify eased up on the free account limitations and put ads in them. But before they did this, they had a well established base.

The story of Spotify is interesting because they did not start with the backing of a big company.* And, at the time, digital music was a contentious topic.

Spotify found new audiences by giving their users something to share (free, legal music), and then requiring new free members to come in through an *existing* member (by invite only). This is classic word of mouth (creating something remarkable, and then enabling influencers).

The reason this worked for Spotify was because they offered something truly valuable. Without breaking the law, you could listen to free music, on demand. And because free accounts only came from those who already had one, it created a club-like appeal.

---

* Even though Spotify did not start with deep financial backing, Daniel Ek, the founder of Spotify, sold an earlier business, Advertigo, and had enough money to retire. However, the point still remains, Spotify did not build its audience through another already established entity, but they built it from the ground up.

creating a marketing strategy

E verything starts here. The tactics you use (or don't use) will change based on your location, the needs of your audience, and the nature of your work. But your strategy is universal. This is the part that will inform the rest of your outreach. You should have a grasp on your marketing strategy well enough to clearly explain it to new employees in the first few seconds.

This chapter walks you through creating that strategy.

two guidelines

Before we get to creating your strategy, there are two things you need to keep in mind. First, simplicity wins. And second, include strategies, not tactics.

Simplicity Wins

If you had to, could you explain your marketing strategy to your audience? Or, what about a seven-year-old? And could you do it in a few seconds?

Complex strategies seem impressive on the surface, but they're usually the ones that get messed up. They have too many moving parts. And the more complicated they are, the fewer people who actually understand them.

By keeping your strategy simple, you maintain what scientists call "elegant." The simpler a concept is, the stronger it is.

Strategies, Not Tactics

Your marketing strategy is a plan that moves you toward your goal. But, like every plan, there will be problems along the way, and you'll need to make adjustments. When you create your marketing strategy, however, try to stay away from tactics, or tools. Tactics can change based on a lot of variables. Strategies, on the other hand, tend to be more versatile.

You will certainly use various tactics when executing your strategy, but the strategy itself will just be the bigger concepts. The reason for this is that you can have a solid strategy, but it may be failing because of the tactics, or tools, you're using with it. However, if you've got a bad strategy, it doesn't matter what tools you use, it will not work.

For this reason, your planning begins with your strategy.

strategic formula

There are three parts to the strategic formula: The first part lays out the overall framework of your marketing. The second part addresses its relevance and drives your ad direction. And the third part is how you will continue to engage with your audience once you've begun.

The three parts can be consolidated into the below three sentences, where you plug in the details in brackets:

We're going to have our [audience] *do our* [objective] *by* [this date] *(or on this* [schedule]*). We are going to engage* [their pain] *with* [our solution]. *And we are going to keep them engaged through* [this procedure].

That's pretty simple. But I've worked with national well-known brands who couldn't fill out those three sentences.

Once you can fill in those blanks, and without jargon, you'll be in a good position to begin putting your strategy into play. Working out those answers is where most of the planning effort of your marketing strategy will come from. Once you understand those answers, the rest, like the tactics, will fall into place.

(You can download the full workbook to walk you and your team through the process at fiveroundrocks.com/resources.)

multiple strategies

You will need as many strategies as you have audiences and objectives. If you have three primary audiences, and you want each audience to accomplish two different things, then you need *six* strategies.

Think of a strategy as a path. Each audience is at a different starting point. They exist in a different place in the world or in life. And they are each looking for different things.

Likewise, your objective is the fork in the road. As you lead your audience down the path, you are asking them to make a decision. Your strategy will encourage your audience to take the right turn at the right time.

Because having multiple strategies can get difficult to keep track of, it's best to start with as few as possible. One, if you can. Pick your most important or impactful target audience, and select just one objective you want them to accomplish.

Starting with one allows you to work out the details of putting a strategy in place. Once you've been working with a strategy and feel comfortable with it, add another. Either pick a second objective for the same target market, or create a strategy for a new target market.

part 1: who does what by when?

The first part—the framework—outlines who your audience is, what you want them to do, and by when. When you begin creating your website and your **calls to action**, it will be directly influenced by this first part.

We're going to have our [audience] *do our* [objective] *by* [this date] *(or on this* [schedule]*).*

Audience

Audience is a general word I've used throughout this book to refer to the specific group of people interested in buying from you. Another term for this is *target market*.

In order to define your audience, think about them in terms of what they have in common. A church, for instance, may define their audience as a group of men and women in their thirties and forties with kids still at home. Or, a retail store who sells dresses from a local designer may define their audience as women in their twenties and thirties looking for something unique and not quite mainstream.

The audience you define is not the only group that will be interested in you, but they are the one you will be specifically *talking* to. Being narrow is a virtue here. The more narrow you are, the more focused your message, and the easier the market will be able to identify you.

Begin by asking yourself: What group naturally aligns with your company?

Objective

Once you know who you are talking to, you next need to determine what you want them to *do*. This is the objective.

In my two examples above, the church's objective is to get their audience to attend services or small group meetings, while the retail store wants their audience to buy their dresses. Your objective should be pretty straightforward.

The difficulty with the objective is not identifying it, but staying with it. Many brands will ask their audience to do a ton of things: like our Facebook page, follow us on Instagram, watch our new promo video, sign up to our newsletter, read a ton of words on our website, and on and on. There is nothing wrong with anything I've just named, it's just that asking for all of these things at once cannibalizes your audience's attention. In other words, they won't know what you really want from them.

Instead of asking them to do all of these things every time they interact with you, you need to isolate the *most important* thing and ask them to do that. (This harkens back to chapter eight's discussion of the sales funnel.)

Timeline

The third thing you need to consider is the timeline. This may start out as a shot in the dark, but it's important that you begin somewhere. Without a timeline, how long are you going to run your ads before you know that they work? And when are you going to know to shift gears because your strategy isn't working? Without a timeline, there's no way to really measure the effectiveness of your strategy.

Once you know your timeline, you're ready to begin plugging in your answers to the first strategy statement.

From my two examples above: *We're going to add ten new families in their thirties and forties to a small group each quarter.* Or:

We're going to sell 30 dresses a week to women in their twenties and thirties. *

At this point, there are usually two areas I hear pushback. First, why does it matter if this exact audience buys in? Shouldn't any audience do fine? And second, this all feels a bit simplistic.

For the audience, you are crafting a system that speaks directly to one specific group. The better you speak to them, the more they will be inclined to listen. This is an issue of scalability. If you don't know *where* your business is coming from (or if you cannot predict it), then you don't have marketing, you've got something more like luck.

And secondly, yes, this *is* simple—by design. You are creating something everyone can instantly understand, because in order to get everyone rowing in the same direction, they need to clearly understand the job. The reason many companies do not have good marketing (and, as a result, do not have a solid brand in the marketplace) is because they are not clear and focused here at the basics.

part 2: what's their pain and how are you solving it?

Once you understand who you are talking to and what you are asking them to do, you need to define what their pain is and how your solution fixes that pain.

---

* I've changed the wording to make it fit, grammatically. That's okay because the concept is exactly the same.

In chapter one, Johnson's audience for their baby washcloths was mothers. The pain they spoke to was a mother's ability to take care of her baby. And their solution is their product, designed to make cleaning your baby pleasant for you *and* your baby.

Part two is the cornerstone of your advertising. Good ads work when they solve a pain point for your audience. Even if you don't plan to buy paid advertising, the message you put out is your 'ad.' And so this part of the marketing strategy addresses that.

We are going to engage [their pain] *with* [our solution].

Their Pain and Your Solution

Begin by thinking about everything you offer to the market. If you have products, this should be pretty straightforward. You do not need to list a full inventory, just group them by their natural categories. If you offer a service, this may be a little more difficult. But still, go ahead and list everything you offer.

Next, make a second list, but on this one include all of your audience's pain points. Not everything on this second list will relate to what you offer and that's okay. What you want to do right here is understand what is on your audience's mind. If you're not sure what their pain points are, there are two ways to find out. First, ask them. Talk to those in your audience you know will give you honest answers. And second, physically walk through their process. When Kim and Mauborgne are training brands to implement a blue ocean strategy, they recommend the team physically imitates what their customers are doing. Many times this will expose hidden pain points you missed before.

Once you have both of your lists, begin by looking at which of your solutions best match up with their pain points. Pick the top one or two. If they are complementary, you can use them both. But keep it as simple as possible.

Following my two examples from before, the second part of the church's strategy may be: *We are going to provide like-minded community with home groups scheduled by other busy parents.* And my dress shop would be: *We are going to keep a steady stream of new styles at affordable prices.*

It's important to remember here, your marketing strategy is *not* your communication strategy. Instead, what you're doing here is getting your facts straight. That way everything you do from here on out can be weighed and measured against this plan.

part 3: what will keep them engaged?

A universal truth of business is that it's easier (and cheaper) to sell to an *existing* customer then it is to acquire a new one. This final part of your marketing strategy lays out how you are going to do that.

When you begin executing this part of your strategy, you may choose to build a sales funnel, incorporate email or social media, or rely on word of mouth. But these are all tactics. They may or may not work, depending on your business model and your audience. What you want to do here is define a natural intersection where you can continue to talk to your existing customers.

And we are going to keep them engaged through [this procedure].

Creating Return Customers

What's less important here is *how* you do this. Many in your audience will simply be amazed that you care enough about them and their experience. There really are few uses of your time and resources that are better spent than checking in with your existing customers.

For my church example, the strategy may look like: *We are going to keep them engaged by regularly talking to them (via phone or text) and by checking to see that they are still involved in their group.* And for my dress company: *We are going to keep them engaged by collecting quarterly feedback from our top customers and annual feedback from any of our other repeat customers through incentives surveys.*

Each of my examples could be done through social media, email, face-to-face interaction, or any other touch point. For the strategic (top) level, you plan to communicate with them to gauge how attached they are to your brand. This is the fundamental purpose of part three. Many brands are happy when they have customers. And they're even happier when those customers come back. But few proactively *monitor* their audience to control the rate at which they do come back.

At this point, some may argue that this is not marketing, it's just good business practices. And it is. But it's also integral to your marketing. Those interactions go into the shaping of your brand's image, and, as such, they perform a key marketing function.

putting it together

The marketing strategy for each of my fictional brands looks like this. For my church:

We're going to add ten new families in their thirties and forties to a small group each quarter. We are going to provide like-minded community with home groups scheduled by other busy parents. And we are going to keep them engaged by regularly talking to them (via phone or text) and by checking to see that they are still involved in their group.

And for my dress company:

We're going to sell 30 dresses a week to women in their twenties and thirties. We are going to keep a steady stream of new styles at affordable prices. And we are going to keep them engaged by collecting quarterly feedback from our top customers and annual feedback from any of our other repeat customers.

Once you've created a marketing strategy, you will now use it as a guide for every touch point between you and your audience. When you buy ad space, put up a post on Facebook, or greet walk-ins, your marketing strategy will serve as your *standard* to know if you are on the right path or not.

But even more than a guide, your marketing strategy will keep your brand focused in spite of a busy and crowded market. Use the worksheet with additional questions at fiveroundrocks.com/resources to complete your marketing strategy.

the end

Any time you create new work that's good, it's hard.

If it wasn't, you would already be doing it. And so would everyone else, for that matter.

The most important part of all of this is to stay encouraged. If you need to take a breather and come back later, do it. If you need to push on through, then do that. And if you're not sure if what you've done is good enough, keep going and put it in action as soon as you can. Once you begin applying your strategy, you'll see what works and what doesn't.

What separates those who succeed from those who don't is not the big things we often compare (like, funding or staff), but it's *perseverance*. Anders Ericsson's 10,000 hour rule (which Malcolm Gladwell made famous in his book, *Outlier*), states that we will achieve world-class performance in an area once we put in our 10,000 hours.

But it's not just clocking 10,000 hours that does it, it's getting 10,000 *focused* hours. Ericsson defines 'focused hours' as including feedback. This way, all subsequent time we spend is better than what came before.

Marketing works the same way. By building a marketing strategy, you'll have a framework that guides your progress. If you experiment, you'll know it's not random, but calculated. And if that experiment doesn't work, you'll be able to adjust it according to your strategy, so that next time, you get closer. By following this process, it won't take long before you move from building a brand new strategy to making minor tweaks and seeing results.

p.s.

One last point of encouragement. Josh Kaufman wrote a fantastic book called *The First 20 Hours*. His thesis is that to get good enough in a new field it only takes twenty hours.

In our world dominated by the 10,000 hours to become an expert, Kaufman's mere twenty hours is a bit of relief.

His twenty hours, however, are not in contradiction to the 10,000 hour rule. On the contrary, he is referring to being *proficient*, while the 10,000 hour rule is about being the best (usually, in the entire world).

But if you've just started your business, or if you run a lean shop, you don't need to be the best in the world. You just need to be good enough to reach your market.

This applies whether we're talking about your website, copywriting, building your sales funnel, or adding elements like gamification to your product or service.

The topics I've included in this book are what successful brands are doing. But they're not exclusive. They don't take special funding, or an abnormally gifted team. Most of them just take some focus and persistence.

glossary of terms

Advertising A specific channel of marketing used to promote a product, service, or brand.

Anchor A mental frame of reference that is used to judge similar values.

Audience Anyone who is (or could be) a recipient to your message. Depending on your business model, it may be a client, customer, member, or donor.

Blue Ocean Strategy Developed by W. Chan Kim and Renée Mauborgne is the process of moving away from "red ocean" competition and into new "blue ocean" markets, through a process of innovation.

Brand General: How your audience experiences your product or service. Specific: The logo, colors, fonts, and associated style that defines your organization.

Brand Ambassador A paid (or unpaid) spokesperson for your brand. This can be an official title, or a spontaneous word of mouth fan. Usually it is the former.

Branding Your visual image, including logo, graphics, colors, and any other visually defining elements.

Buyer Utility Map A blue ocean tool that uncovers which 'levers' you can adjust to better focus on your audience's pain points.

Call to Action The primary objective you want your audience to accomplish.

Consumption Vocabulary Words that describe the benefit of using a product. Specifically, this refers to pre-purchase descriptions.

Content Marketing Providing quality content for free in order to build trust with your audience.

Copywriting Writing that prioritizes generating more customers about other factors (style, form, or other objectives).

Cost What you give up to create a product or service. (Compare to *price* below.)

Curse of Knowledge Confusing your audience by using a summary statement when your audience is not familiar with the background story or equivalent examples.

Downward Forces The elements of a sales funnel that motivate your audience to move further down the funnel.

Fans Individuals who like your product and will tell others on a one-by-one basis. (Compare to *Influencers* below.)

Flat Marketing A nonstrategic approach to marketing centered around advertising.

Flow A state of concentration (and enjoyment) where time seems to disappear.

Focus A laser-sharp point that takes priority over everything else.

Gamification Applying the elements and design of game (in non-game setting) to a product or service to make its use more desirable.

Goldilocks Zone When the target option is framed next to a too-little and a two-much option.

Heuristics A mental shortcut. Our brains prefer to think of familiar thoughts rather than new (or hard) ones.

In Medias Res A Latin phrase that refers to the middle of the action or story.

Influencer A person or brand who already has an established platform.

Integral Marketing A strategic form of marketing that begins with (and often informs the creation of) a product or service built specifically for your audience.

Landing Page A page online created especially for an ad or promotion that is extremely focused. It may have the components of a sales letter. It can be a page on your website, or a third-party service.

Long Tail A statistical term for the range of a distribution curve that has many offerings but low volume of each offering.

Loss Aversion When the fear of losing is greater than the reward of gaining the same amount.

Market (person) The group most likely to buy your product. Broader than target market (below).

Market (place) The place where you sell your products or services.

Marketing The systematic process of getting the right message to the right audience.

Marketing Strategy The plan you put in place and test your marketing results against.

Mere Exposure Effect Building audience trust by subtly and repetitively showing them something many times.

Minimalist Marketing People-first marketing that relies on brands building trust and personalized relationships with their audiences.

New Audiences A different type of audience with potential to buy from you, but who currently do not. Similar to the "non-customer" of blue ocean strategy.

Path to Purchase Each buyer goes through a five-step process when deciding to buy or re-buy.

Pioneer-Migrator-Settler Map A blue ocean tool that helps you compare how the market is receiving your current offerings.

Price What your audience gives up to receive your product or service. This often includes money. But it may include (or even be limited to) time, energy, or a competing product or service. (Compare to *cost* above.)

Product In general: the value you provide to your audience. In specific: a tangible value, as opposed to an (intangible) service.

Public Relations Managing a brand's public image, often in response to negative issues.

Publicity The process of putting your message in front of broad audiences, some of which may be New Audiences.

Rhetoric The art of verbal persuasion.

Sales Funnel The intentional process of moving individuals in your audience from not-buying to buying.

Scarcity The force that increases attention when important resources are limited.

SEO Abbreviation for "search engine optimization," the process of making your website easy for search engines (specifically google) to find.

Service An intangible value provided to your audience.

Story (in business) A framework that illustrates the problem, solution, and success of your product or service.

Strategy Principles that are always in play and apply to everything you do.

Strategy Canvas (also called **As-Is Canvas**) A blue ocean tool that helps you compare your primary competition to your own offerings.

Tactic Tools used to execute a strategy.

Target Audience The specific group of your audience that you are speaking *directly* to. More narrow than your market (above).

Target Product The product or service you want to sell most. Will often be accompanied by a lower and higher wing product.

Value When benefit outweighs cost.

Value Cost Frontier A blue ocean tool for reexamining what **value** means to your market.

Viral When Word of Mouth sharing happens at an exponential rate.

Viral Coefficient The formula that determines how many of your current customers must share your work (and subsequently how many of those who it is shared with must become new customers) for your message, brand, or product to be considered "viral." See chapter twelve for the formula.

Wing Products Products or services created to steer your audience toward your target product.

Word of Mouth When customers voluntarily (and *without* compensation) advertise on your behalf.

recommended reading

Below are the books I recommend for taking these ideas further. They're listed by category, then alphabetical by author. The one or two bolded titles in each category are a good place to start.

psychology / sociology

Anderson, Chris. *The Longer Tail.*

Ariely, Dan. *Predictably Irrational.*

Ariely, Dan and Jeff Kreisler. *Dollars and Sense.*

Cialdini, Robert. *Influence.*

Cialdini, Robert. *Pre-Suasion.*

Csikszentmihalyi, Mihaly. *Flow.*

Eagleman, David. *Incognito.*

Ericsson, Anders and Robert Pool. *Peak.*

Goleman, Daniel. *Focus.*

Kahneman, Daniel. *Thinking, Fast and Slow.*

Mlodinow, Leonard. *Subliminal.*

Mullainathan, Sendhil and Edgar Shafir. *Scarcity.*

Surowiecki, James. *The Wisdom of Crowds.*

Taleb, Nassim Nicholas. *The Black Swan.*

marketing

Adams, Scott. *Win Bigly.*

Berger, Jonah. *Contagious.*

Dib, Allan. *The 1-Page Marketing Plan.*

Goden, Seth. *All Marketers Are Liars.*

Goden, Seth. *Free Prize Inside!*

Goden, Seth. *Ideavirus.*

Goden, Seth. *Permission Marketing.*

Goden, Seth. *Purple Cow.*

Goden, Seth. *Tribes.*

Heath, Chip and Dan. *Made to Stick.*

Holiday, Ryan. *Growth Hacker Marketing.*

Pulizzi, Joe & Robert Rose. *Killing Marketing.*

Ries, Al and Jack Trout. *Positioning.*

Ries, Al and Jack Trout. *The 22 Immutable Laws of Marketing.*

Ries, Al and Jack Trout. *Focus.*

Rohrs, Jeffrey K. *Audience.*

Schaefer, Mark. *Known.*

Sernovitz, Andy. *Word of Mouth Marketing.*

Sweetwood, Adele. *The Analytical Marketer.*

Thompson, Derek. *Hit Makers.*

Werbach, Kevin and Dan Hunter. *For the Win.*

Zichermann, Gabe and Joselin Linder. *The Gamification Revolution.*

business

Behar, Howard. *It's Not About the Coffee.*

Brunson, Russell. *Expert Secrets.*

Fried, Jason and David Heinemeier Hansson. *Rework.*

Guillebeau, Chris. *The $100 Startup.*

Hyatt, Michael. *Platform.*

Kahn, Barbara. *Global Brand Power.*

Kaufman, Josh. *The First 20 Hours.*

Kim, W. Chan and Renee Mauborgne. *Blue Ocean Strategy.*

Kim, W. Chan and Renee Mauborgne. *Blue Ocean Shift.*

Port, Michael. *Book Yourself Solid.*

Ries, Eric. *The Lean Startup.*

Snow, Shane. *Smartcuts.*

Stanley, Andy. *The Principle of the Path.*

Thiel, Peter. *Zero to One.*

Weinberg, Gabriel and Justin Mares. *Traction.*

communication

Clark, Roy Peter. *Writing Tools.*

Cron, Lisa. *Wired for Story.*

Edward, Ray. *How to Write Copy That Sells.*

Heinrichs, Jay. *Thank You for Arguing.*

LeFever, Lee. *The Art of Explanation.*

Miller, Donald. *Building a Storybrand.*

Snyder, Blake. *Save the Cat!*

sales

Adamson, Brent, Matthew Dixon, Pat Spenner, and Nick Toman. *The Challenger Customer.*

Hogshead, Sally. *Fascinate.*

Hogshead, Sally. *How the World Sees You.*

Iannarino, Anthony. *The Only Sales Guide You'll Ever Need.*

Ogilvy, David. *Confessions of an Advertising Man.*

Pink, Daniel. *To Sell is Human.*

Rackham, Neil. *S.P.I.N. Selling.*

Voss, Chris. *Never Split the Difference.*

resources

All tools and guides from this book can be downloaded at at:
fiveroundrocks.com/resources

website themes

StoryBrand theme
Church theme
Service theme
Retail theme
Nonprofit theme
Influencer theme
(And we're regularly adding more)

blue ocean tools

Strategy Canvas
Buyer Utility Map
Pioneer-Migrator-Settler Map
Strategy Canvas
New Value Cost Frontier
3 Tiers of Noncustomers

marketing guides

Step by Step Guide to Writing a Profitable Sales Funnel
Marketing Strategy Worksheet
5 Ways to Know When Your Marketing is Not Working
How to Get (and Write) Winning Testimonials
(And others)

acknowledgments

I have been privileged to work with many great clients, and this is where I have undoubtedly learned the most.

I am grateful to everyone who has helped me with this project. Sam and Gary, for your design input. Wes, for your support and encouragement. Stacey (mom), for taking off your 'mom' hat and putting on your 'editing' hat. And Kristin, for trying your best to keep me from saying dumb things in public. I appreciate that the most.

For all the mistakes still here, these are, unmistakably, my own.

research

introduction: focus
AMA's definition of marketing can be found at https://www.ama.org/AboutAMA/Pages/Definition-of-Marketing.aspx.

chapter 1: focus
"Full absorption in what we do" is from Daniel Goleman's book *Flow*, page 22.

On finding flow. As a side note, flow can come in all shapes. I like to write. And when do, I use an application called Scrivener. It helps keep me organized, and I can see my entire book in outline form at a glance. For me, that's a big help. I also listen to music, which helps with the external distractions. And I put my computer on do-not-disturb so that emails or text messages don't distract me. When I've got a block of time (usually an hour or more) this scenario has become a way for me to manufacture flow in my own process. Not only is it enjoyable, but it is highly productive.

"After we invest effort" is from Dan Ariely and Jeff Kreisler's book, *Dollars and Sense*, page 115.

The IKEA effect was coined by Michael I. Norton (Harvard Business School), Daniel Mochon (University of California, San Diego), and Dan Ariely (Duke University) in their paper "The IKEA Effect: When Labor Leads to Love," published in the Journal of Consumer Psychology 22, no. 3 (2012), pages 453-460.

"Deep concentration...1 percent" is from Leonard Mlodinow's book, *Subliminal*, page 35. The next two quotes ("categorization is a strategy" and "mental database of cultural norms"), also come from Mlodinow, pages 145 and 191, respectively.

"Brain...does not need to know" is from David Eagleman's book, *Incognito*, page 28.

"Leaders aren't even aware" is from Chip and Dan Heath's book, *Made to Stick*, pages 255-256.

The Long Tail discussion is from Chris Anderson's book, *The Long Tail*, and the three forces are from pages 52-57.

chapter 2: value

"The 'romance of leadership'" is from Robert Cialdini's book, *Pre-Suasion*, page 66.

Regarding the benefits of being special, Jonah Berger, professor of marketing at The Wharton School at the University of Pennsylvania, defines another factor of special: remarkability. In his book Contagious he notes: "Remarkable things are defined as unusual, extraordinary, or worthy of notice or attention." But the engine behind remarkable is that it provides social currency. "They make the people who talk about them seem, well, more remarkable," writes Berger. "Sharing extraordinary, novel, or entertaining stories or ads makes people seem more extraordinary, novel, and entertaining" (39).

"Easiest way to get into a person's mind" is from Al Ries' and Jack Trout's book, *Positioning*, page 19.

"Act of creation is singular" quote is from page 1 of of Peter Thiel's book, *Zero to One*.

Regarding statistics on marketshare. As always, with statistics you can tell about any story you wish to find. The data here comes from https://www.netmarketshare.com and https://www.idc.com, respectively. Https://www.statistica.com shows similar figures.

Some conflicting viewpoints will highlight two additional factors. First, the total market share of Microsoft includes all of their operating systems on the market (e.g. Windows XP, 7, 8, 10, etc.). Second, market share does not consider how much are purchased in a year, but instead how much are active. Meaning, one of the two may in fact be trending in a direction current market share does not show.

Another point to consider is the difference between the mobile and desktop markets. Windows does not own ~90% of all platforms, just the desktop platform. Irrespective of brand, the mobile market worldwide has overtaken the desktop market (however, in the United States, the desktop market still holds more market share—roughly 50% vs 40%— than the mobile market). See gs.statcounter.com/platform-market-share/desktop-mobile-tablet/ for more information on different regions.

Another important tangent is that Apple does do a better job of monetizing their brand than Microsoft. Their earnings reports show them clearly outpacing Microsoft. But this is actually a red herring to the discussion of market share, because market share is a representation of how many people want a product, not how well the owner of that product makes money.

Blue Ocean Strategy comes from W. Chan Kim's and Renée Mauborgne's books *Blue Ocean Strategy* and *Blue Ocean Shift*. The quote come from *Blue Ocean Shift*, page 145.

chapter 3: communication

The movie dialog is from *Office Space*, Twentieth Century Fox, 1999.

"Your nervous system responds" is from an article by Mary C. Lamia on Psychology Today, https://www.psychologytoday.com/blog/intense-emotions-and-strong-feelings/201012/it-or-not-emotions-will-drive-the-decisions-you.

The story of Eliot's tumor is from *The Sydney Morning Herald*, http://www.smh.com.au/national/feeling-our-way-to-decision-20090227-8k8v.html

"He was utterly detached" quote is from Lisa Cron's book, *Wired for Story*, p 45-46.

System 2 is explained more in Daniel Kahneman's book, *Thinking, Fast and Slow*, p. 20-21.

The seven-part framework is Donald Miller's from his book, *Building a Story Brand*.

"No matter how beautiful your website is" was from a Ramit Sethi email on December 4, 2017.

How to Write Words that People Want to Read section is largely based on Ray Edwards' book, *How to Write Copy That Sells*.

"8 out of 10 people will read a headline" is from copyblogger.com's ebook, *How to Write Magnetic Headlines*, p. 49.

The Bluma Zeigarnik story comes from Robert Cialdini's book, *Pre-Suasion*, p. 86-87.

Classic advertisement for Lion Matches can be found at https://bestcopyads.wordpress.com.

A diamond seller. Jeff Sexton writes in a March 14, 2011 article on Copyblogger.com about the example of how copywriter Roy H. Williams used this technique for a diamond seller:

> *Antwerp, Belgium, is no longer the diamond capital of the world.*
> *Thirty-four hours on an airplane. One way. Thirty. Four. Hours. That's how long it took me to get to where eighty percent of the worlds diamonds are now being cut. After 34 hours I looked bad. I smelled bad. I wanted to go to sleep. But then I saw the diamonds.*
> *Unbelievable. They told me I was the first retailer from North America ever to be in that office. Only the biggest wholesalers are allowed through those doors. Fortunately, I had one of 'em with me, a lifelong friend who was doing me a favor.*

Now pay attention, because what I'm about to say is really important: As of this moment, Justice Jewelers has the lowest diamond prices in America, and I'm including all the online diamond sellers in that statement.

Now you and I both know that talk is cheap. So put it to the test. Go online. Find your best deal. Not only will Justice Jewelers give you a better diamond, we'll give you a better price, as well.

I'm Woody Justice, and I'm working really, really hard to be your jeweler. Thirty-four hours of hard travel, one way. I think you'll be glad I did it.

"The ad starts off by setting up an open loop," Sexton notes. "If Antwerp is no longer the diamond cutting capital of the world, which city is the new one? But we're not told which city; we're only strung along with the hint that it takes a 34-hour plane trip to get there."

The ad concludes without ever revealing the name of this city. This is walking the line. Williams is a master copywriter and he pulls it off. But if you don't close the loop, your marketing will have the opposite effect: you'll turn off your audience.

chapter 4: direction

Classic Xerox machine study by Ellen Langer from https://www.psychologytoday.com/blog/brain-wise/201310/the-power-the-word-because-get-people-do-stuff.

"The art of persuasion." While Heinrichs' definition works well in the context of his book, I limit the definition of "rhetoric" in this book to "the art of verbal persuasion." This is still consistent with what Heinrichs teaches. But as the rest of this chapter will illustrate, there are other nonverbal ways to persuade.

Seven techniques to use rhetoric effectively come from Jay Heinrichs' book, Thank You for Arguing, pp. 218-19, 227-28, 237, 248, 259, 270, and 278.

"The experience of familiarity" quote is from Larry Jacoby in Daniel Khaneman's book, *Thinking, Fast and Slow*, p. 61.

"Words that you have seen before," and subsequent quotes come from Daniel Kahneman's book, *Thinking, Fast and Slow*, pp. 61, 62, and 66.

"8 x 7 x 6 x 5 x 4 x 3 x 2 x 1" is from Chris Voss's book, *Never Split the Difference*, p. 130.

"System 1 understands sentences" is from Daniel Kahneman's book, *Thinking, Fast and Slow*, p. 122-23.

Nicholas Epley and Thomas Gilovich's paper, "Putting Adjustment Back in the Anchoring and Adjustment Heuristic: Differential Processing of Self-Generated and Experimenter-Provided Anchors," from the journal, Psychological Science 12 (2001), p. 391-96.

"When their mental resources are depleted" and following quotes are from Daniel Kahneman's book, *Thinking, Fast and Slow*, pp. 121 and 160-161.

"We should try to repay" quote is from Robert Cialdini's book, *Influence*, p. 17.

Hare Krishna Societiy's success is from Robert Cialdini's book, *Influence*, p. 24. And as a note here, society eventually caught up and some laws were changed and others became more aware of the tactic, preventing the Krishnas from being so aggressive. Until this happened though, their system functioned as a veritable goldmine.

Victim experiment and statistics come from Robert Cialdini's book, *Influence*, p. 59-60.

"When we are unsure of ourselves" quote is from Robert Cialdini's book, *Influence*, p. 129.

"Liking is where it starts." Well, I just quoted myself. I try not to be one of those pretentious people, but, sometimes, it's unavoidable. So I buried it here in the notes. Here's the original article: http://joefontenot.info/how-to-spot-con/.

"We buy more from salespeople who are similar to us" and subsequent
quotes in this section all come from Robert Cialdini's book, *Influence*,
pp. 171, 204, 167, and 171,

"By guiding preliminary attention strategically" and subsequent references
to the six commanders of attention come from Robert Cialdini's book,
Pre-Suasion, pp. 132, 55, 64, 69, 73, 78, 83, 87-88, and 92-95.

2014 study on the subtlety of associations is by Xiao Chen and Gary P.
Latham's article, "The Effect of Priming Learning vs. Performance Goals
on a Complex Task" in journal, Organizational Development and
Human Decision Processes 125, p. 88-97.

The Thinker experiment detailed in Robert Cialdini's book, *Pre-Suasion*, p.
104.

"brands were chosen by 47 percent of the audience" quote is from Robert
Cialdini's book, *Pre-Suasion*, p. 144.

chapter 5: scarcity

"What happens to our minds" quote and subsequent quotes from the
"Bandwidth Tax" section are from Eldar Shafir and Sendhil
Mullainathan's book, *Scarcity*, pp. 12 and 51.

$80 million revenue from https://www.forbes.com/sites/michelinemaynard/
2013/09/22/how-starbucks-turned-pumpkin-spice-into-a-marketing-
bonanza/#14b311e5718a.

Pumpkin Spice Latte black market from 6 https://www.theatlantic.com/
business/archive/2014/10/the-company-that-tested-out-pumpkin-spice-
foie-gras-mashed-potatoes/381192/.

chapter 6: gamification

U.S. Army gamification in the mall from http://americasarmy.com.

80% of businesses statistic comes from Brian Burke's Forbes article at
https://www.forbes.com/sites/gartnergroup/2013/01/21/the-
gamification-of-business/#528f91d94dc2.

"Gamification is a process" quote comes from Gabe Zichermann and Joselin Linder's book, *The Gamificiation Revolution*, p. 153.

"Track behavior, keep score" quote comes from Gabe Zichermann and Joselin Linder's book, *The Gamificiation Revolution*, p. 19.

"Dopamine drip of constant feedback" quote comes from Kevin Werbach and Dan Hunter's book, *For the Win*, p. 73.

All subsequent quotes—except for "introducing a letterboard alone," which is from Webach and Hunter's *For the Win*, p. 73—come from Zichermann and Linder's *Gamification Revolution*, pp. 20, 21, 22, 159, and 160.

chapter 9: price

Drazen Prelec's MIT experiment from Dan Ariely's book, *Predictably Irrational*, p.26-29.

"Tendency to be anchored by extreme numbers" quote is from Chris Voss's book, *Never Split the Difference*, p. 130.

"We contemplate buying a product or service" quote is from Dan Ariely's book, *Predictably Irrational*, p. 30.

"we choose from among descriptions" and subsequent quote come from Dan Ariely and Jeff Kreisler's book, *Dollars and Sense*, pp. 154 and 156.

chapter 11: word of mouth

"What all of these [remarkable] companies have" quote is from Seth Goden's book, *Purple Cow*, p. 20.

"A free prize is the essence" and subsequent quote are from Seth Goden's book, *Free Prize Inside!*, pp. 19 and 21.

chapter 12: new audiences

Box office bust data comes from https://en.wikipedia.org/wiki/List_of_box_office_bombs.

Viral Coefficient equation comes from Gabriel Weinberg and Justin Mares's book, *Traction*, p. 121-123.

Facebook user stats are for December 2017 and come from https://
newsroom.fb.com/company-info/.

Spotify user states come from seekingalpha.com/article/4160286-spotify-
unique-ipo-dynamics.

about the author

Joe is a marketing and communication consultant.

In 2016, he founded the marketing firm, Five Round Rocks, which helps entrepreneurs and nonprofits build marketing that works. And he is the marketing strategist for one of the largest seminaries in the world.

Visit **fiveroundrocks.com/subscribe** to get regular articles on building your business.

Joe lives in New Orleans with his wife, Kristin, and their two kids, Graham and Hadley.

If you found this book helpful, please leave it a review on Amazon. That's huge.

And if you'd like to reach me directly, my email is joe@fiveroundrocks.com. I'd love to hear from you.

Made in the USA
Columbia, SC
11 January 2019